Computer Wings

IT TroubleShooter

Course Book

Syllabus Version 1.0

First Edition 2009

ISBN 9780 7517 5758 3

British Library Cataloguing-in-Publication Data
A catalogue record for this book is available from the British
Library

A joint publication from:

Q-Validus Ltd.

NovaUCD   t: + 353 1 716 3741
Belfield Innovation Park   e: info@computerwings.com
University College Dublin   w: www.computerwings.com
Dublin 4   w: www.q-validus.com
Ireland

BPP Learning Media Ltd

BPP House, Aldine Place   t: 0845 0751 100 (within the UK)
London W12 8AA   t: + 44 (0) 20 8740 2211
United Kingdom   e: learningmedia@bpp.com
                            w: www.bpp.com/learningmedia

Computer Wings® is a registered trademark of Q-Validus Limited in Ireland and other countries. This Computer Wings approved Course Book may be used in assisting Candidates to prepare for their Computer Wings certification test.

Candidates wishing to sit Computer Wings certification tests are required to pre-register for the programme. Candidates may register at any Authorised Centre.

Without registration no certification tests can be taken and no Computer Wings certificate or any other form of recognition may be awarded.

For any further information about Computer Wings visit www.computerwings.com

This Computer Wings IT TroubleShooter Course Book is dedicated to the memory of Dr. Michael Sherwood-Smith.

CONTENTS

1 CONCEPTS

2 CONNECT

3 OPERATING SYSTEM

4 INSTALL

5 ADMIN

What is Computer Wings?

Computer Wings is an exciting new practical computer skills certification programme for real world tasks and roles in the modern workplace.

The certification delivers real world skills in a range of areas. Computer Wings assures increased efficiency, higher standards of output, greater levels of collaboration, and improved user confidence.

The Computer Wings programme covers the key functions within an organisation such as planning, project management, communication, marketing, IT, online business and process flows.

The Computer Wings programme is a flexible, modular based scheme, allowing candidates to select the module or modules which are most appropriate to their current or future job roles.

Computer Wings provides a total programme solution, including registration, automated testing and certification, as well as supporting training materials.

For any further information please visit www.computerwings.com

Scottish Qualifications Authority (SQA) endorsement

The Computer Wings qualification scheme is mapped to the UK National Occupational Standards (NOS) and is endorsed by the Scottish Qualifications Authority (SQA). The Computer Wings programme has been credit rated and levelled for the Scottish Credit Qualifications Framework (SCQF).

IT TroubleShooter has been officially designated as SCQF level 7 with 9 credit points. To see the SCQF level and credits for all other Computer Wings Modules visit http://www.computerwings.com/endorsements

Get certified

You now have your Computer Wings Course Book, which is designed to bring your skills to the next level. The next step is to prove your competencies by taking the Computer Wings certification test. Computer Wings is endorsed by the Scottish Qualifications Authority (SQA) www.sqa.co.uk, a world renowned awarding body.

Register for your test

To gain your Computer Wings certification you need to register for your test with a Computer Wings Authorised Centre.

Computer Wings certification tests are only available through Authorised Centres. For further information visit www.computerwings.com

Computer Wings overview

Computer Wings is an exciting new computer skills training and certification programme. The programme consists of ten stand alone modules which focus on the productivity skills required in today's rapidly changing economy.

The Computer Wings certification programme comprises the following modules:

Project Manager

Plan, resource, execute and manage mid-sized projects to deliver high quality, well defined, organised results on time and on budget.

Mail Manager

Communicate and collaborate more effectively by becoming expert in the use of email software to manage organisational scheduling and communication.

Diagram Maker

Enhance effective business communication by using diagram tools and image editing applications to create diagrams, images and conceptual schemes.

Newsletter Publisher

Produce professional quality newsletters, brochures, eshots or leaflets to support marketing activity and organisational communications.

Presenter Pro

Enhance business communications by developing the skills to create and deliver attractive, persuasive and audience focused presentations.

Web Creator

Create and maintain informative and user-friendly websites to support internal and external communications.

Web Optimiser

Develop Search Engine Optimisation (SEO) skills to support and improve website traffic, create more impact and generate higher sales.

Web Analyser

Use website analysis tools to measure the appeal of a website, see the origin of visits and referrals, and generate reports about website activity.

IT TroubleShooter

Develop the IT administration skills required to deal with hardware, software, memory and network issues in small IT network environments.

IT GateKeeper

Recognise important software, hardware and network security considerations in order to protect small IT network environments.

Computer Wings benefits

The Computer Wings certification programme enables the Candidate to develop their skills and confidently address computing applications relevant to their needs.

The Computer Wings certification programme delivers:

- A recognised and valuable qualification.

- Practical skills, competencies and knowledge.

- Awareness of good practice, efficient and productive use of applications.

- Confidence to produce effective and well crafted outputs.

- High return on human and capital investments.

- Validation of skills and knowledge as evidenced by certification.

- A match between Candidate skills and organisational needs.

- Enhanced collaboration skills in the organisation.

- Improved productivity through more efficient use of office applications.

- Professional looking outputs.

- Enhanced communication across the organisation.

Content validation

Q-Validus works with Subject Matter Experts (SME) globally, as well as renowned international awarding bodies and international partners, to develop and provide Computer Wings, which reflects a comprehensive and recognised skills and knowledge standard.

Computer Wings Course Books are developed by SME's across the range of specialist domains, including end-user computing, Internet and IT.

Ongoing content validity of Computer Wings Syllabus standards definition is maintained by the Syllabus Expert Group (SEG) using the Q-Validus online Content Validation Database (CVD), a bespoke software tool for standards validation. Expert feedback and comments from around the world, in respect of Computer Wings Syllabus measuring points is collated and recorded in the Content Validation Database. The current Computer Wings Syllabus Version is Syllabus Version 1.0. The ongoing standards validation process for Computer Wings supports the continuing applicability and relevance of Computer Wings.

Experts wishing to provide technical comments and feedback in relation to Computer Wings Course Books, or seeking to participate as experts in relation to the Computer Wings Syllabus standards definition, should contact: technical@computerwings.com

Computer Wings IT TroubleShooter overview

Computer Wings is an internationally recognised computer and ICT skills standard. Computer Wings training and certification programmes help Candidates work more effectively by developing computer and ICT skills that deliver valuable productivity benefits.

Computer Wings IT TroubleShooter is a certification in the area of network administration. The core Operating System (OS) products referenced in this Course Book version are Microsoft XP and Microsoft Vista.

The Computer Wings IT TroubleShooter certification validates Candidate skill and knowledge in administering small IT network environments.

Candidates shall:

✓ Understand common computer hardware terms and concepts such as memory, motherboard, Central Processing Unit (CPU), BIOS.

✓ Distinguish between different kinds of software; applications software, Operating System (OS) software, utility software.

✓ Recognise hardware and software compatibility issues, and the role of software drivers.

✓ Understand the term network as it is used in computing, and the terms bus and network hub. Recognise different network cable types, and the concept of a wireless network.

✓ Recognise different kinds of network connections (PSTN, ISDN, ADSL, DSL).

✓ Understand the concept of IP addressing on the Internet and different Internet protocols (TCP / IP, HTTP, HTTPS, FTP).

✓ Be able to install hardware and software, and configure browsing software securely.

✓ Install; upgrade different operating systems.

✓ Adjust desktop settings and apply user or organisational profiles across a network.

✓ Troubleshoot user accounts and permissions across a network.

✓ Prepare a client computer for use, setting permissions, mapping drives, applying ant accessibility features.

✓ Apply a partition to a drive.

✓ Understand the term backup, and implement appropriate backup and restore routines.

✓ Be able to administer and troubleshoot peripheral devices such printers, monitors, modems and external storage media.

✓ Understand how data protection, copyright issues, health issues and disability legislation relate to using computers in the organisation, and promote appropriate policies.

IT TroubleShooter syllabus

Category	Skill area	Ref.	Measuring point
9.1 CONCEPTS	9.1.1 Hardware	9.1.1.1	Understand basic hardware concepts.
		9.1.1.2	Select and connect different IT system components such as CPU (Central Processing Unit) box, monitor, keyboard and mouse.
		9.1.1.3	Understand the main internal components of a computer such as: memory, motherboard, Central Processing Unit (CPU).
		9.1.1.4	Understand the concept of Central Processing Unit (CPU) speed.
		9.1.1.5	Understand the term BIOS.
	9.1.2 Software	9.1.2.1	Understand basic software concepts.
		9.1.2.2	Understand the term operating system (OS) and what its function is.
		9.1.2.3	Identify different kinds of applications software.
	9.1.3 Memory	9.1.3.1	Understand different kinds of memory: RAM, ROM, cache.
		9.1.3.2	Understand the terms tracks, memory sectors, memory clusters.
		9.1.3.3	Know what fragmentation is and what it is caused by.
	9.1.4 Compatibility	9.1.4.1	Know what is meant by compatibility issues between hardware and software.
		9.1.4.2	Know where to access information about known compatibility issues (eg technical forums; manufacturers' website).
9.2 CONNECT	9.2.1 Networks	9.2.1.1	Understand the term network.
		9.2.1.2	Understand the term bus, and its role.
		9.2.1.3	Understand the term network hub.
		9.2.1.4	Identify different types of network cables: coaxial, twisted pair, fibre optic.
		9.2.1.5	Understand the concept of a wireless network.
	9.2.2 Connections	9.2.2.1	Distinguish different kinds of connectors: SCSI, USB, Bluetooth etc.
		9.2.2.2	Know different connection types: ISDN, ADSL, DSL etc.
		9.2.2.3	Understand the term modem and its function.
		9.2.2.4	Recognise the requirement for login and password details to access an ISP (Internet Service Provider).
		9.2.2.5	Understand the network terms: client / server.

Category	Skill area	Ref.	Measuring point
	9.2.3 Internet	9.2.3.1	Distinguish between the Internet and the WWW (World Wide Web).
		9.2.3.2	Distinguish the term Internet from Intranet.
		9.2.3.3	Understand the terms LAN (Local Area Network), WAN (Wide Area Network), VPN (Virtual Private Network).
		9.2.3.4	Understand the concept of IP addressing and its purpose.
		9.2.3.5	Understand the term firewall and what purpose it serves.
		9.2.3.6	Understand the terms URL and DNS, and explain them.
		9.2.3.7	Know the most common protocols: TCP / IP, HTTP, HTTPS, FTP, IPX / SPX.
9.3 OPERATING SYSTEM	*9.3.1 OS Types*	9.3.1.1	Recognise the most common operating systems.
		9.3.1.2	Know different ways to install an operating system: by downloading from the Internet, from a network, installing from a CD.
		9.3.1.3	Recognise a file or directory system is an operational platform for a network.
	9.3.2 Setup	9.3.2.1	Know how to install, upgrade an operating system.
		9.3.2.2	Know how to create a startup disk.
		9.3.2.3	Use a GUI to map drives, create shortcuts, and manage desktop icons.
		9.3.2.4	Set up a VPN client.
		9.3.2.5	Set up desktop configuration with different themes, backgrounds, taskbar orientations etc.
		9.3.2.6	Recognize different file types: application files, temporary files, system files etc., and know where they might be stored.
		9.3.2.7	Understand what the boot menu is.
		9.3.2.8	Understand how to partition a hard drive.
		9.3.2.9	View available hardware and its configuration.
	9.3.3 Performance	9.3.3.1	Start the computer in safe mode.
		9.3.3.2	Monitor server performance.
		9.3.3.3	Obtain the IP address for a computer (i.e. PING a server).
		9.3.3.4	Use network software to monitor network, hardware, software performance, memory usage rates.
		9.3.3.5	Monitor and analyse system events log.

Category	Skill area	Ref.	Measuring point
	9.3.4 Backup	9.3.4.1	Know the purpose of backing up.
		9.3.4.2	Know how to schedule a backup, restore backup.
		9.3.4.3	Know how to check (verify) a backup.
		9.3.4.4	Know different media types for backing up. Know about rotational backup schemes, and the importance of off-site backups.
		9.3.4.5	Know the meaning of the term surge protector.
		9.3.4.6	Understand UPS and what it is used for.
9.4 INSTALL	*9.4.1 Printers*	9.4.1.1	Identify different printer types: dot matrix, laser, ink jet.
		9.4.1.2	Be able to install different printers.
		9.4.1.3	Know how to add, modify and remove a printer.
		9.4.1.4	Control permissions for a shared printer.
		9.4.1.5	Cancel, pause, re-start a print job.
		9.4.1.6	Be able to troubleshoot everyday printer problems.
		9.4.1.7	Be able to replace printer consumables and clean printers.
	9.4.2 Monitors	9.4.2.1	Recognise different monitor types. Identify factors which can impact display quality such as resolution, refresh rate, number of colours used.
		9.4.2.2	Be able to install different monitors.
		9.4.2.3	Know how to change settings such as resolution, refresh rate, number of colours displaying.
		9.4.2.4	Connect an overhead projector to a local machine.
	9.4.3 Peripheral Devices	9.4.3.1	Install a modem, or other communications device.
		9.4.3.2	Install different peripheral devices such as scanners, CD ROM drive, additional memory, memory expansion cards, sound cards, network interface cards.
		9.4.3.3	Be able to install different plug 'n' play devices.
		9.4.3.4	Be able to add different assistive technology devices.
		9.4.3.5	Recognise that all components consume power.
		9.4.3.6	Recognise that cleaning peripherals helps maintain efficiency.

Category	Skill area	Ref.	Measuring point
	9.4.4 Software	9.4.4.1	Be able to install internet browser, email software.
		9.4.4.2	Be able to install applications software.
		9.4.4.3	Be able to install different utility software (backup, diagnostic, antivirus).
		9.4.4.4	Be able to remove different kinds of applications software.
		9.4.4.5	Install, remove , or maintain different device, network driver sets.
9.5 ADMIN	*9.5.1 Settings*	9.5.1.1	Change mouse, keyboard settings.
		9.5.1.2	Change regional settings, language settings.
		9.5.1.3	Be able to add or remove fonts etc.
		9.5.1.4	Adjust accessibility settings.
	9.5.2 Email	9.5.2.1	Configure email software.
		9.5.2.2	Install and setup a simple mail server setup.
		9.5.2.3	Set up email accounts, webmail accounts.
		9.5.2.4	Understand and configure different network protocols.
	9.5.3 Accounts	9.5.3.1	Set up a new user group.
		9.5.3.2	Modify permissions for a user or for a user group.
		9.5.3.3	Add, remove users to / from a group.
		9.5.3.4	Install, configure and remove network services.
		9.5.3.5	Access usage details, user details, logon time, passwords, membership etc.
		9.5.3.6	Create common resources, files, printers.
		9.5.3.7	Troubleshoot user access / permissions issues.
		9.5.3.8	Know good password policies.
	9.5.4 Anti-virus	9.5.4.1	Understand the term virus and the main virus types: Trojan horses, viruses, worms etc.
		9.5.4.2	Be aware of various laws and guidelines that are applicable.

Category	Skill area	Ref.	Measuring point
9.6 LAWS & GUIDELINES	9.6.1 Issues	9.6.1.1	Be aware of data protection legislation or conventions in your country with regard to data storage and use.
		9.6.1.2	Be aware of copyright laws and their impact for downloading content from the Internet, using licensed software. Understand the concept and impact of software piracy.
		9.6.1.3	Know about health issues when users interact with the computer such as ergonomic issues, posture, lighting, taking regular breaks.
		9.6.1.4	Know about safety issues when using computers such as having secure cabling, adequate ventilation, protecting against fire hazards, eye care with screen and monitor usage.
		9.6.1.5	Recognise the significance of disability / equality legislation in helping to provide all users with access to computers.

Concepts

Hardware 2

Software 9

Compatibility 10

Concepts

Connect

Operating system

Install

Admin

Measuring points

- Understand basic hardware concepts
- Select and connect different IT system components such as CPU (Central Processing Unit) box, monitor, keyboard and mouse
- Understand the main internal components of a computer such as memory, motherboard, Central Processing Unit (CPU)
- Understand the concept of Central Processing Unit (CPU) speed
- Understand the term BIOS
- Understand basic software concepts
- Understand the term Operating System (OS) and what its function is

- Identify different kinds of application software
- Understand different kinds of memory; RAM, ROM, cache
- Understand the terms tracks, memory sectors, memory clusters
- Know what fragmentation is and what it is caused by
- Know what is meant by compatibility issues between hardware and software
- Know where to access information about known compatibility issues (eg technical forums; manufacturers' website)

Introduction

Computing is based on how physical hardware and application software of various kinds combine to perform a whole range of tasks, services and operations.

In this chapter, the basic concepts of hardware (the physical parts of a computer), software (the applications that run on computers) and compatibility (ensuring the hardware and software can work together) are covered. Knowing what these concepts are and what they refer to will help you better understand how computers and networks operate.

Microsoft Windows XP is one of the predominant Operating System (OS) products currently in use. This Course Book references Windows XP in its example and action sequences to illustrate the text and support the training objectives of the Syllabus. References and illustrations for Windows Vista are also provided.

Hardware

Hardware refers to the physical components of the computer and any other peripheral devices that are used with it.

This includes:

- The box in which the circuits, drives etc. are placed.

- The circuitry, microchips and the board on which they sit.

- The hard drive.

- The monitor and keyboard.

- Other peripheral devices, which are not essential to the computer itself, but are essential to its use, such as a printer, monitor or an external media drive.

Main components of a computer

In this section, the essential hardware that allows your computer to function properly is covered.

Memory

Memory is the physical storage medium for computers.

Computers need memory for three reasons:

1. To maintain information that is being used for applications.

2. To load instructions to enable the computer to work.

3. To store information that can be called up again and changed.

These three uses are met by three different types of memory:

- *Random Access Memory (or RAM):* stores information temporarily for applications that are running as illustrated.

- *Read Only Memory (or ROM):* stores instructions that tell the computer how to work.

- *Storage Media:* which is where the files you save are kept.

In this section these concepts are examined in more detail.

Random Access Memory (RAM)

RAM is a chip that stores information that can be read, written to, deleted or modified.

RAM is considered volatile memory, which means the information on it can be lost easily. If there is a power outage, any information stored in RAM will be lost.

RAM is used to store information for the computer's Operating System (OS) and any applications that are running. It allows the computer user to add, alter and modify information. An example of this is a Microsoft Word document. When you are working on the document, it is stored in RAM. This is where you add, delete or modify the information in the document. However, the document can only be stored in RAM temporarily. Once an application is closed, RAM will drop any of the unsaved information it has related to the application. This is part of the reason why applications prompt you to save a copy of your work to a permanent drive if you try and close a working file without saving it.

Another aspect of RAM is cache memory. Cache memory is part of RAM. Cache is a store for frequently read data. The computer will check cache memory first so that the data can be accessed quickly.

Some of the key characteristics of RAM are:

- It is a chip.

- It is volatile.

- Information stored on it can be read, written to, modified or deleted easily.

- Information is stored on it temporarily.

- It is used to store information for the computer's OS and any applications it is currently running.

Read Only Memory (ROM)

ROM is a chip that stores information that cannot be added to, deleted or modified.

ROM is considered as non-volatile memory, which means the information stored on it cannot be easily lost. Even if there is a power loss, the information stored in ROM will remain.

ROM memory is used to store and run instructions that are read when the computer starts up. The instructions stored in ROM at startup is the BIOS or Basic Input Output System. The BIOS instructs the computer about the hardware and devices of which it is comprised and how communications will work between the devices.

It is important that ROM cannot be written to as changing these important startup instructions could make the computer unstable and/or unusable. The BIOS will be discussed in more detail later.

Some of the key characteristics of ROM are:

- It is a chip.

- It is non-volatile, which means information on it cannot be lost easily.

- Information stored on it cannot be written to or modified easily.

- Information is stored on it permanently.

- It is generally only used to store system-critical data, or information that is essential for the computer to run properly.

Storage

Storage is the memory where files are kept for later use.

Storage memory allows files to be read, written, overwritten and deleted. In general, you work on current information in RAM, then save it to some form of storage media, a hard drive in the computer itself, a network, or to a removable media format. Storage memory is considered non-volatile, as files stored there will remain after a power failure. However, stored files can become corrupted (for example, by malicious software), be overwritten or lost.

Different storage media is used to maintain files on your computer or network. Storage is generally considered distinct from other kinds of memory (ROM and RAM). These kinds of memory are used in the operation of the computer, and are typically located on the motherboard. Storage on a computer refers in the first instance to the hard drive, but also to external drives, tapes, USB keys, as well as CD's or DVD's which are used to archive data.

The characteristics of storage are:

- It can be a disk or a chip.

- It can be removable or non-removable.

- Information on it can be read, or written. Information on hard drives, removable drives and USB keys can also be overwritten or deleted. This is not the case with CDs and DVDs.

- Information stored on it is kept for long periods of time.

Motherboard

> A motherboard is the physical board that the computer's essential components are affixed to. The components are connected to each other through circuitry that runs through the board.

The motherboard allows the computer's Central Processing Unit (CPU) to communicate with the other components. The CPU is discussed in more detail in the next section.

Generally, the motherboard will physically hold essential components, with other devices being added to the computer through connectors. However, some non-essential devices may be added directly to the motherboard, because they are increasingly important to more modern computers. Examples of these include video and sound cards. While they are not essential to the running of the computer, the increase in multimedia information (and the use of sounds in applications for warnings, etc) has increased their importance.

Central Processing Unit (CPU)

> The Central Processing Unit (CPU) is considered the computer's 'brain'. It performs the calculations and steps through the logic of program instructions that are at the heart of the computer's operation.

The CPU is a chip that processes information for the computer.

Fundamentally, every computer action is performed as a calculation. Whether the computer is processing information it receives from hardware (for example, keyboard strokes), or executing an action defined by a piece of software for example, displaying text on screen, it does so by processing a series of bits and bytes in a defined manner and the CPU performs these calculations.

The CPU has two distinct parts:

- *Arithmetic Logic Unit (ALU)*: performs arithmetical and logical operations.

- *Control Unit*: takes instructions from the memory (ROM or RAM) and processes them using the ALU.

CPU speed

A measure of a CPU's performance is its speed. The faster a CPU is, the more calculations it can perform. The more calculations it can perform, the faster the computer will run.

The speed of a CPU is known as its clock rate. Computers process information as bits, which are a series of 1s and 0s. The clock refers to how long it takes for the CPU to change between a "1" state and a "0" state. The clock rate refers to how many changes of state (or cycles) can be made in a second. The CPU clock rate is measured in hertz, a measure of electrical frequency. To give an example, early computers had CPU's with a clock rate of 2 Megahertz (MHz). This would perform 2 million cycles per second. More recent CPU's have clock rates of 2 Gigahertz (GHz), which can perform 2 billion cycles per second.

Overclocking means attempting to force the CPU to work faster than it was designed or intended to work. This activity is usually only undertaken by specialists who may have a particular technical interest in the processing capacity of the CPU.

Overclocking can cause the computer to freeze, which can mean information that was being worked on is lost.

Basic Input Output Services (BIOS)

The Basic Input Output System (BIOS) is a set of instructions that tells the computer how to communicate with and use essential hardware on the computer. The BIOS also launches the computer's Operating System (OS).

The BIOS prepares the computer for use by providing a set of instructions to enable the different physical components to work together.

When a computer is switched on, the ROM will run the BIOS. This makes the computer aware of attached components so that it knows how to execute commands from software. The BIOS will also launch the Operating System (OS), which allows other software, such as applications, to be run and understood by the computer.

The BIOS is invisible to the computer user and generally, it is inaccessible

Hard drives

> The hard drive is the computer's non volatile, permanent physical data storage area, where computer files are stored and retained even when the machine is switched off.

Hard drives are usually magnetic disks, with a device called a read/write head. The read/write head writes to and reads from the disk to store and retrieve files.

The disk itself is divided into tracks, sectors and clusters:

- A sector is the smallest section of the physical disk where information is stored.

- Each hard disk is composed of a series of sectors organised into circular sections. These circular sections are known as tracks.

- A cluster is a collection of sectors that hold information related to the same file or process.

A single sector holds up to 512 bytes of data. Even if the data to be stored on a sector is less than 512 bytes, no other data is written to the sector. In most cases, information is written to many sectors. For efficiency, the computer will try to store the information into several sectors that are situated beside each other. Such a collection of sectors is called a cluster.

At the same time, files cannot always be stored into continuous sectors in this way. This can occur because the next sector beside a cluster is being used to store other data. When this occurs, the computer will locate the next available sector and store information there, repeating the process until the whole file has been stored. This process increases efficiency in the short to medium term. However, over time, files that are continually edited can become slow to respond, as data relating to them is stored in several clusters that are in different locations on the disk. To remedy this, a defragmentation software tool can be used.

Fragmentation

> Fragmentation is the splitting up of the various parts of a computer file, through repeated save and delete operations, across different regions of a disk.

Defragmentation is the process of identifying data from the same file that is stored in different locations on the hard drive and moving it so that all the file information is arranged more closely together.

Because data is often stored in different locations across the hard drive, when you want to open a file, the computer must find each fragment and put it together again. This requires the computer's read/write head on the drive to work harder than if all the information were stored more closely together. This has two effects; as file sizes get larger, or more files are stored on your computer, the computer can become slower to respond. Secondly, there is physical wear and tear on the hard drive's read/write head, reducing its lifespan.

By taking these fragments of data and placing them closer together, the defragmentation tool will improve your computer's performance and improve the life of your hard disk.

Fragmentation is more of an issue where larger files or databases are in use. However, it is still good practice to regularly defragment a hard drive to keep it working efficiently. Also, should the hard drive crash, it will be easier to recover data on a disk that has been regularly defragmented.

You should plan to defragment your hard drive as a separate maintenance task.

Use the following steps to defragment your hard drive in XP:

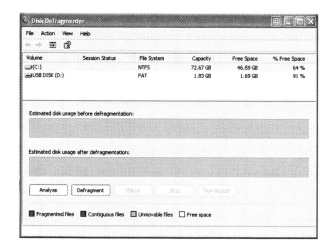

Actions

▸ 1. Click *Start*, select *Programs*.

▸ 2. Click *Accessories*, select *System Tools* and select *Disk Defragmenter*.

 Windows Vista also has a Disk Defragmenter and it is accessed in a similar way.

The *Analyze* button will scan the computer for fragmented files to identify whether defragmentation of the hard drive is necessary.

The *Defragment* button will start the defragmentation process. It is good practice to allow the process to complete its processing routine once you have started it. There are various reports associated with disk defragmentation which can be viewed and produced.

Software

Introduction

> In computing, software is a term used to cover all types of programs that are used with computing systems.

There are two broad types of software:

- Systems software: this software runs the computer using the OS software, or other tools called utilities.

- Applications software: this software is used to perform specific tasks, like word processing or doing calculations.

Operating System (OS)

> The Operating System (OS) is the software that manages the resources and controls the operations of the computer.

The OS manages, schedules and controls the resources of the computer. It also allows the computer's hardware and software to communicate and enables the computer to be part of a network.

The tasks an OS performs include:

- Recognising and processing inputs (for example, keystrokes on a keyboard).

- Processing user data and outputting it appropriately (for example, displaying information on a screen).

- Running applications.

- Ensuring all applications have enough resources to run efficiently.

- Managing file systems and data storage.

- Ensuring hardware added to the computer is recognised.

- Maintaining security on the computer.

- Networking with other computers and/or servers.

Operating systems are generally divided into categories as follows:

- *Multi-user*: allows several people to run applications at the same time.

- *Multi-processing*: where an application runs using more than one CPU.

- *Multi-tasking*: where more than one application runs at the same time.

- *Multi-threading*: allows multiple parts of the same application to run at the same time.

- *Real time*: allows the computer or system to respond to real life events as they occur.

Applications software

> Applications software is a set of programming instructions used to carry out a task.

Application software is developed for use with specific system level software, such as your computer's OS. The application will communicate with the OS in order to use the computer's resources and other devices. Application software is developed for a wide range of purposes, from writing documents or creating spreadsheets, to playing video clips and browsing the Internet.

Sometimes, applications software is bundled together in what is known as an applications suite. An example of this is Microsoft Office or Open Office, which both provide a range of software tools that help computer users in organisations to improve their communication (for example, by using email), collaboration (for example, by using shared documents and calendars) and productivity (for example with databases and spreadsheets).

Compatibility

> Compatibility measures how well hardware and software work together.

For software and hardware to work together, they need to know how to communicate and use each other's resources.

Compatibility is usually divided into two categories:

- Software compatibility: is when a piece of software works with other relevant software and the computer.

- Hardware compatibility: is when different hardware devices and the device driver software (software which helps devices work with the computer) interact appropriately with the computer.

Software compatibility issues arise when:

- An application will not work with the OS.

- An upgrade to software means that older versions of the software cannot work with the data created by the new application (this is known as backwards compatibility).

- Two applications cannot communicate with each other.

To prevent software compatibility issues, you should ensure any software you buy is compatible with the computer's OS. You should also implement software upgrades for all computers at the same time. Where there is no backwards compatibility for a software upgrade, manufacturers will often release application readers. An applications reader will allow you to view the information created by the upgraded software. The best place to find out about these kinds of tools is on the developer's website.

Hardware compatibility issues arise when the computer will not work with a newly installed peripheral device. A typical example of this occurs when you plug a printer into the computer, and it will not work.

In most cases, you need to install the driver software so that the OS will be able to recognise and work with the new hardware. Manufacturers often release driver software with their hardware for this reason, or make it available for download on their website. By going to the manufacturer's website, and searching under the specific product code or reference, you can generally find the required driver software.

Drivers

A driver is software that works to communicate between an Operating System (OS) and a peripheral device.

For any peripheral device to work, (printer, monitor, modem etc.) it needs to follow its own set of instructions contained within its driver software. It needs to interpret standard commands, for example to print three pages from a word processing application, and then relay these commands through its driver to make the printer actually work.

Manufacturers continually update their drivers to make them faster, more reliable and more stable. Most OS's include a range of drivers for standard devices. However, if you buy a piece of hardware that is newer than your computer or has been updated in some way, you will typically need to install the driver for it. Generally, drivers are delivered with the device on a CD or included as part of the USB device installation. Also you can usually download drivers from the manufacturer's product website.

Plug and Play hardware

'Plug and Play' was developed by Microsoft as a universal technology to help make adding hardware devices much simpler when working with computers and to help reduce compatibility problems.

Enabling the Plug and Play technology in Windows XP and Vista are thousands of software drivers for the most common hardware devices. The driver is the software code which allows a particular hardware device, for example a printer, to be compatible with the computer and take instructions from the OS to carry out the various applications and printing tasks.

Device manufacturers often make the software drivers for their hardware peripherals available to Microsoft and other vendors as soon as they become available. Also with the Windows Update online service, it is quite simple to find a device driver which may not be installed with your current Windows OS version.

Even given the planning and thought which goes into making peripheral devices interact with computers and networks, compatibility issues are still a common technical support query. There is usually a simple reason as to why device compatibility is a problem, and often it is based on product or software releases and their compatibility. For example:

- Older Device: with an old peripheral device, there may not be an XP or Vista driver version provided or available which will allow the device to continue to work with a new OS.

- Newer device: with a new peripheral device, the driver may not yet be supported by Windows.

Compatibility planning

To help avoid compatibility issues for peripherals when working with XP or Vista, it is best to keep a few points in mind before you plug anything in.

First, try to find out by searching on the Internet to check if the drivers exist for your device. Many device manufacturers may have a special driver downloads section on their websites to help with this.

It is also worth adding that the same principle applies when upgrading an older machine with a new OS. You should check with the manufacturer that the specification of the new machine will function properly given the demands of the new OS.

Microsoft maintain a very useful resource, the Windows Catalog Website: http://www.microsoft.com whdc/hcl/default.mspx, where you can check if hardware is listed and if a driver is available.

For Windows Vista, Microsoft have a Certified for Windows Vista logo which helps users easily identify those devices which offer standard compatibility with Vista.

Finding drivers

If you have a device, but not its driver, you will need to find an appropriate driver for the device.

With new devices, it is possible that the driver is already included with the OS. However, before you try to install the device you should check the packaging and/or manual.

If you do not have a CD or USB key with the driver, usually delivered with the device, you will need to download the driver from the manufacturer's website, or from the Windows Update Catalog website.

Windows update catalog

Microsoft maintains a special area for third party device drivers within their Windows Update Catalog website visit http://www.windows.com/downloads

The *Windows Update* service maintains an up-to-date version of Windows OS driver additions. *Windows Update* will check if updates are required for the computer and add when necessary on restart.

In Vista and XP *Windows Update* can also be accessed by clicking *Start*, selecting *All Programs* and selecting *Windows Update*. This will open your Internet browser on the Windows update page: http://update.microsoft.com

Hardware manufacturer's website

You can also visit the manufacturer or product websites directly to find hardware drivers. However, it is important to ensure the drivers you download are compatible with your OS. As a second security measure, you should check that the drivers have passed the Windows Logo testing to ensure they have met the compatibility requirements.

Many manufacturers will release beta divers for public download. 'Beta' is a term for software that is being released, but has not yet passed a rigorous testing process. Often, software is released as Beta so that users can report back any problems they encounter. However, in the context of hardware drivers, it makes sense to avoid using Beta drivers, as they can cause unforeseen problems with your OS.

Driver compatibility warning

In XP and Vista warning messages display during installation when drivers do not pass compatibility testing. For example, if you are attempting to use a Windows 2000 version driver with a common printer under the XP OS, a warning message may display. The best approach is to heed the warning message and try to find the latest driver for the newer OS from the device manufacturer's website or from Microsoft. Working with an outdated driver version may also cause other problems.

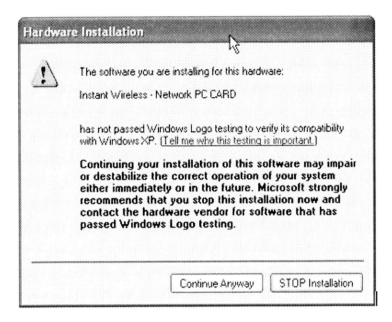

Drivers on third party websites

There is a whole range of websites devoted to helping you find device drivers.

Many include features like a forum or a discussion board, and often these can help if you are trying to solve a particular driver device compatibility issue.

These kinds of websites can be useful, especially if you have a particular query, for example will a printer manufacturer continue to support an older version driver as the latest version OS emerges?

Other forum users may have come across your problem, and may be in a position to help with some advice, or indeed a generic driver for a device which is no longer being manufactured or supported. As a word of caution using these kinds of generic device drivers should always be considered carefully. Ideally certified drivers from the manufacturer in question are the best approach.

It is worth noting that third party driver websites can also lead to downloading additional products or files that may be harmful to your computer.

The only way to ensure your computer continues to run smoothly is to use certified drivers from trusted sources.

Quick Quiz

Select the correct answer from the following multiple-choice questions:

1 Which one of the following is a component of a CPU?

   a   ALU

   b   RAM

   c   Cache

   d   SCSI

2 What is BIOS?

   a   An essential set of routines that starts up the computer.

   b   The expansion of physical memory onto the hard disk

   c   A component of the CPU that processes calculations

   d   Part of the motherboard controlling video display and colour settings

3 What is multi-threading?

   a   Running a program on more than one computer

   b   Running more than one program concurrently

   c   Running different parts of a single program concurrently

   d   The use of a program by two or more users at the same time

4 How much data can be held on one sector of a hard disk?

   a   128 bytes

   b   256 bytes

   c   512 bytes

   d   1024 bytes

Answers to Quick Quiz

1   a   ALU

2   a   An essential set of routines that starts up the computer

3   c   Running different parts of a single program concurrently

4   c   512 bytes

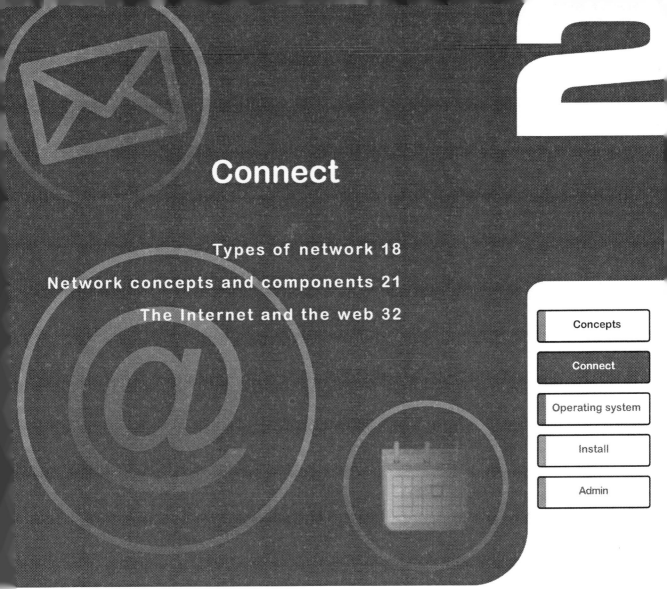

Connect

Concepts

Connect

Operating system

Install

Admin

Measuring points

▸ Understand the term network
▸ Understand the term bus and its role
▸ Understand the term network hub
▸ Identify different types of network cables: coaxial, twisted pair, fibre optic
▸ Understand the concept of a wireless network
▸ Distinguish different kinds of connectors: SCSI, USB, Bluetooth etc
▸ Know different connection types: ISDN, ADSL, DSL etc
▸ Understand the term modem and its function
▸ Recognise the requirement for login and password details to access an ISP (Internet Service Provider)
▸ Understand the network terms: client/server

▸ Distinguish between the Internet and the WWW (World Wide Web)
▸ Distinguish the term Internet from Intranet
▸ Understand the terms LAN (Local Area Network), WAN (Wide Area Network), VPN (Virtual Private Network)
▸ Understand the concepts of IP addressing and its purpose
▸ Understand the term firewall and what purpose it serves
▸ Understand the terms URL and DNS
▸ Know the most common protocols: TCP/IP, HTTP, HTTPS, FTP, IPX/SPX

Introduction

This chapter covers the fundamental concepts of networks within computing. The chapter examines the different network types and configurations used, the physical network connectors and different infrastructure. The internet protocols associated with different network types are also covered.

Networks allow computers and other devices to communicate, share information and use common resources. The development of networks in organisations has brought a marked increase in the productivity of organisations, as people can communicate and collaborate easily.

Types of network

A network is a collection of computers or other devices linked together so they can communicate. Each computer or device on the network is called a node.

Each node sends and receives information through a piece of hardware designed specifically for communicating data. This hardware can be called a network card, Network Interface Controller (NIC) or LAN adapter. Historically, there were a range of technologies used to connect computers and devices to a network. However, since the early 1990s Ethernet technology has been used as a de facto standard. Each node on an Ethernet network has a unique Media Access Control (MAC) address. The MAC addresses for devices are purchased from an organisation called the Institute of Electrical and Electronic Engineers. This means that the MAC address for any piece of network equipment is truly unique.

There are many types of computer network, from small office based networks, to international networks supporting a global business, to city wide networks. Some of the most common networks are as follows:

- Local area networks (LANs): where the computers are geographically in close proximity.

- Wide area networks (WANs): involves connecting two or more networks together over large distances using telecommunications links.

- Campus area networks (CANs): where the computers are confined to a specific geographic area, such as a college campus.

- Metropolitan area networks (MANs): a computer network designed for an urban centre such as a town or city.

- Home area networks (HANs): a network contained within the home allowing a user to connect to a range of devices.

LANs and WANs

The most common networks are LANs and WANs. These are used by organisations to facilitate communication between their computers and other devices.

LAN

A LAN is a network of computers and devices which are physically close together.

LANs connect computers within the organisation using physical cables (or wireless connections).

LAN networks are generally used in an office environment to allow users to:

- Communicate using email, or chat.
- Share information by sending it directly, or using a common network repository.
- Share devices, for example, printers.
- Share software.

Larger organisations, like banks, may have LANs that span a number of buildings. However, the buildings are usually close together (within one kilometre). Some large organisations segment their LANs by department.

LANs can be implemented in a number of ways. They are generally differentiated by their:

- Topology: the arrangement of computers and devices that allows them to communicate.
- Protocols: the rules and computer code they use to communicate and share information.
- Media: the physical cabling (or wireless) connection used to allow communication and collaboration.

Each of these aspects of the LAN will determine how fast it can send information between computers and devices.

WAN

A WAN connects computers, devices and even other networks over a large geographic area. A WAN will often connect devices across city, country or even regional boundaries.

The best known example of a WAN is the Internet, which connects networks across the world.

WANs are used to provide communication links between computers, devices and networks that are geographically dispersed.

The infrastructure and cabling used to create the WAN can be owned by an organisation to connect regional offices. However, they are more typically owned by a phone company or network infrastructure business.

WANs can connect users in different ways, based on specific protocols and physical connections. These include:

- Leased lines: which allow an organisation to rent cabling between two offices.

- Circuit switching: which creates a dedicated connection between two points (for example, ISDN connections).

- Packet switching: which is where information is broken up into discrete pieces called packets, sent across the WAN and reassembled by the receiver.

- Cell relay: which breaks information into discrete pieces of a pre-defined length called cells. This connection offers higher quality than packet switching, but requires greater resources.

The method of connecting to the WAN will determine the cost of connection, speed of information flow and security of the information sent across the WAN.

The development of networks has seen a growth in Virtual Private Networks (VPNs), which offer secured, private communication over public cabling and infrastructure. Many organisations use VPNs to create their own inter-office WANs.

Wireless networks

Wireless networking allows computers and other devices to communicate without using physical cables to connect them.

Wireless connections are made using electromagnetic waves, such as radio waves or microwaves. These connections can be made using Wi-Fi, cellular or satellite links.

Wireless networks are becoming increasingly popular, as they reduce the need for cabling, which can become confusing and difficult to administer as more nodes are added to the network. They also allow people to access information while they are away from their organisation's

or WAN. This has increased productivity by extending the ability of users to communicate and collaborate while travelling or working remotely.

Wireless networks need to be secured to prevent unauthorised interception of communications or access to network resources and/or information. This is achieved by encrypting the information sent across wireless networks and blocking access to networks. The Wi-Fi Protected Access 2 (WPA2) key is used to do this. This acts like a password, preventing unauthorised persons from using the network and encrypting the information sent across it. However, the WPA2 key does not encrypt information sent and received by remote workers who are connecting to a local network over the Internet. In these cases, a VPN or other encryption method is required to protect the information being transmitted.

Wireless LAN

A well known type of wireless network is the Wireless LAN (or WLAN) found in organisations and homes. This type of wireless network typically uses Wi-Fi to connect computers and devices in the network.

WLANs are generally restricted to a specific physical area, like an office or building.

Fixed wireless data

Fixed wireless data connections connect networks in two separate locations. This type of wireless network connection is often used to connect WLANs in two buildings owned by the same organisation. This allows an organisation to streamline its ability to communicate, collaborate and increase productivity without the expense and logistical requirements of using physical cables to connect the buildings and the networks within them.

Network concepts and components

Introduction

In this section, some of the important concepts of networking, the different architectures used, as well as their components are covered.

Bus

A bus is a physical cable that connects to all the computers and other devices in the network.

When computers are connected together by a bus, it is known as bus architecture.

The diagram below illustrates a bus network, with each node connected to a main cable (also known as a backbone).

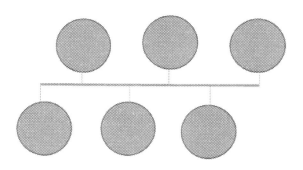

Information sent across a bus network is sent to every device on the network, but only the intended recipient will actually read and process it. If a device fails, the network can continue to operate as normal. The network will only stop working if the bus cable itself is severed. As the network grows, it can become less efficient, as a lot of network traffic is generated, even in simple communications.

Bus Network

Ring

In a ring network, each computer or device is connected to two other devices (one on either side).

The diagram below illustrates a ring network, with each node connected to two other nodes, one on either side of it.

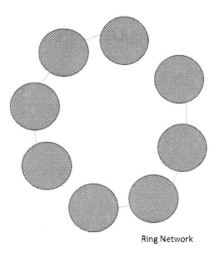

Ring Network

Information is sent through the network in one direction, either clockwise or anticlockwise. Each device passes on the information to the next device until the communication reaches the intended recipient. The drawback of this is that if one device fails on the network, the whole network will no longer operate. Also, adding computers or devices requires careful planning, as the network requires some amount of reconfiguration.

Star

In a star network, each computer or device is connected to a central hub.

The diagram illustrates a star network, with each node connected to the hub.

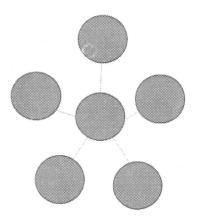

Star Network

The hub manages communication between devices by receiving and sending information from and to devices on the network. The hub itself can be one of three different devices: a hub, switch or router. These will be covered in more detail later.

Stars are the most common type of network in organisations. They require more cabling than a bus network, but can be scaled more easily. Also, if a connection or single device fails, the network can continue to operate as normal. However if the hub fails, the whole network will stop working.

Tree

A tree network is a combination of multiple star networks, connected using a bus cable.

Usually, each star network hub connects to the bus.

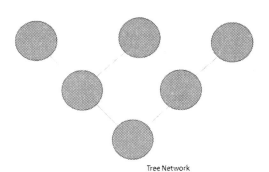

Tree Network

The diagram illustrates a tree network, with each hub connected into a central bus.

This type of network provides excellent scalability with the ability to add more devices or hubs to the network.

Mesh

A mesh network is where each computer or device is connected to several other computers or devices.

There are two types of mesh network:

- Fully connected (or full mesh): is where each computer or device is connected to every other computer or device.

- Partially connected (or partial mesh): is where computers and devices are connected to several other nodes.

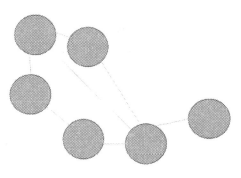

Mesh Network

Full mesh networks are not practical to implement, as they are both costly and complex. Providing a direct link from every node to every other node requires a lot of cabling.

Partially connected networks allow information to be sent by routes from one network node to another. The information is generally sent by the shortest path from sender to receiver. However, if one node is down or not operational, the information can take another path to reach the intended recipient. The internet is a form of mesh network.

Network hub

A hub functions as a connection point for devices on a network. Hubs have a series of ports and enable data transmission over the network.

Each node on the network is connected to the hub through a port. When a computer wants to communicate with another computer or device, it sends the message to the hub. The hub then forwards the information to the recipient.

A hub has two functions: listening and broadcasting. It listens through all its ports for any incoming information. When it receives information, it broadcasts it to all the other ports.

Information sent from one computer is received by all the other computers or devices attached to the hub, whether they use the information or not.

The information itself will usually include an address, so that the intended recipient knows to read the information. Other devices, seeing the information is not intended for them ignore the information.

When more computers are added to a network, using hubs to share information becomes more difficult, as computers become bombarded with information being shared. For this reason, hubs are typically used for small or home networking.

How does a hub work?

Data is transmitted over a network in 'packets'. These are discrete pieces of the message being sent that are assembled by the recipient in order to read the message. The hub takes these packets and forwards them to the recipient. Hubs, switches and routers all deliver data in different ways.

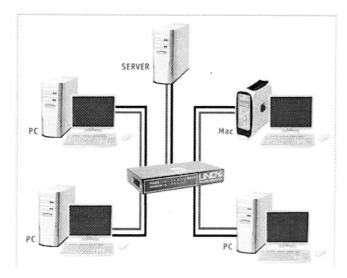

Switches

> A switch is a more intelligent device than a hub, in that it can direct information through a specific port.

If you have six computers attached to a switch, computer A can send information to computer C without also sending the same information to computers B, D, E, and F. If you imagine a group of houses in a village, this is like a neighbour dropping a note into a specific house.

This makes networking more efficient as information is only sent to the intended recipient. Switches are used more than hubs in modern computer networks.

Routers

> Routers are even more intelligent devices and could be considered small computers, dedicated to sending information to computers on other networks or subnets (smaller groups of computers on a network).

A router maintains a list of addresses for computers and networks, so it does not need to be connected to a specific computer to send information to it.

It can also be programmed to decide the best way to send information to a computer. In our example of a group of houses in a village, the router is like the local post office. Not only does it know the location of any specific house anywhere in the village, it can also send post to houses in other towns, cities or countries.

Network cables

Network cables work by carrying electrical (or light) signals over wires. In the case of cables carrying electrical signals, it is important to ensure the wires are properly insulated to ensure electrical signals are not lost, or pick up interference from electrical devices close to the cable.

Coaxial

> Coaxial cable has an inner conductive 'core', which carries a signal. This is covered by a layer of insulation. The insulation is surrounded by another conductive layer, which acts as a shield, protecting the inner core from electrical interference. The final layer is a thick jacket, which protects the cable from weathering and other damage.

Coaxial cable is perhaps best known as the cable used to connect TVs to a cable network or satellite.

However, telephone companies also use this type of cable to transmit information because the outer shield protects the inner conductor from electrical interference that could degrade the data being transmitted.

Coaxial cable can be used to connect computers on a local network, (although cost implications sometimes mean that twisted pair cabling is used more often for this purpose). Coaxial can also be used to carry data over long distances, for example from a local network to a WAN. However, the introduction of fibre optic cables has meant most coaxial cabling is still primarily used to carry television signals.

Twisted pair

Twisted pair cabling consists of two insulated wires that are twisted around each other.

Twisted pair cabling was widely used to carry telephone signals. It is still commonly used to connect computers and other devices on a network.

In a twisted pair cable, there can be multiple twisted pairs, all carrying signals.

There are two types of twisted pair cabling:

- Unshielded twisted pair.

- Shielded twisted pair.

In unshielded twisted pair cabling, the twisted pairs rely on their own insulation to prevent interference. With shielded twisted pair, the pair is insulated with plastic.

Unshielded twisted pair is generally used to connect computers and devices on a network, as this form of cabling is reliable enough to carry signals over a short to medium length. It is also much cheaper than coaxial or fibre optic cabling.

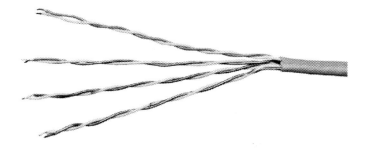

Fibre optic

Fibre optic cable uses a glass or plastic core to carry light signals that represent data.

Fibre optic cable is increasingly used to develop the infrastructure that connects organisations and homes on a city, regional, national and even international basis. It can also be used in local networks, but the cost and effort required to implement such cabling means most small networks still use twisted pair cabling.

In a fibre optic cable, light is transmitted and kept within the cable using a process called total internal reflection. This prevents loss of data over long distances.

Fibre optic cabling has a number of advantages over traditional cabling, which transmits data using electrical signals:

- It is not subject to electrical interference, making it more reliable over long distances.

- Greater bandwidth can be achieved than in traditional cabling. This has proved vital as more information is sent and received worldwide.

Connectors

A connector is the physical interface used to allow devices to communicate with each other.

In this section, three common types of connectors: SCSI, USB and Bluetooth are examined.

SCSI

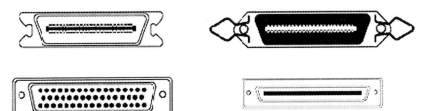

Small Computer System Interface (SCSI) is a set of standards that defines how computers communicate directly with other devices.

SCSI interfaces are used both within a computer, to connect components on a motherboard and also to add peripheral devices, like printers, monitors or external drives, etc.

There are a variety of SCSI connectors available. They generally consist of a series of pins, which fit into a corresponding series of receptacles. Information travels through these connectors between devices. However, the number of pins in a SCSI device varies widely, as the standard defines a method of transmission, rather than the physical connection that is made.

SCSI connectors allow multiple devices to be attached to a computer, in a 'daisy chain' fashion. This means each device is plugged into another, with some device being connected to the computer. However, the connection to the computer allows the computer to control and communicate with any device connected in the chain.

USB

Universal Serial Bus (USB) is a more recent standard for connecting computers and peripheral devices. It is intended to replace SCSI and other connection standards to provide a single, simple connection between computers and other devices. It cannot yet reach the speed of the fastest SCSI interfaces, but offers greater flexibility.

The USB standard is used for most Plug and Play devices. Many USB devices can be used by a computer without requiring a restart, which is not possible with the SCSI interface. Many will also allow you to use a device without having to install manufacturer specific drivers.

Bluetooth

Bluetooth is a wireless connection that uses radio waves to transmit information over short distances between computers and other devices.

It is particularly popular with smaller, battery powered devices, such as mobile phones and laptops. It is commonly used to synchronise the information held on a personal device, like a PDA, with a laptop or desktop computer.

However, Bluetooth can be used for other purposes, such as wirelessly connecting a printer or other mobile phone device to a computer. It also allows multiple devices to connect together.

Connection types

This section deals with some of the different connection types that allow a computer or network to access the Internet and communicate with other computers or networks.

ISDN

> ISDN (Integrated Services Digital Network) is a communications method for sending digital signals across the public telephone network.

ISDN was developed to improve the quality and speed of phone lines carrying voice and data signals.

Traditional phone lines using the Public Switch Telephone Network (PSTN) make dial up connections to the Internet. These transmit data using analogue signals. Analogue is slow and prone to interference. Using a dial up connection also means that phone calls cannot be made at the same time as data is being transmitted.

ISDN addresses these issues by allowing digital signals to be transmitted over phone lines. An ISDN cable is divided into channels, by sending information at distinct frequencies. Each channel can carry information at a specific speed. This means voice information (for example, someone talking on a phone) can be carried at the same time as computer data (for example, someone accessing the Internet). ISDN is a circuit switched connection, which means it creates a dedicated line between the sender and receiver over which it sends information.

There are two types of ISDN:

- Basic Rate Interface, (ISDN BRI): is the most common type of ISDN connection. This has two 64Kb/s channels, which can carry information.

- Primary Rate Interface, (ISDN PRI): operates in the same way, but adds more channels, which allows faster transmission speeds. The number of channels offered on ISDN PRI differs across countries. However, to give an example, the US has 23 channels and Europe 30.

An ISDN connection is faster than dialup, but slower than broadband connections. ISDN became a popular method to connect to the Internet when people wanted faster connections than dialup would provide, but broadband was still expensive and not widely available. It is now in decline, as broadband services become increasingly available and more affordable.

DSL

Digital Subscriber Line (DSL) is a family of technologies that provide digital communications over the telephone network.

DSL is commonly known as broadband. It was originally developed to extend the speed and reliability of ISDN connections.

By using high frequencies to transmit information, DSL allows a large amount of data to be sent across a telephone line at the same time. DSL technology can also subdivide the frequency that it sends data on. This allows multiple computer connections, as well as voice and fax transmission to occur at the same time. To split the cable in this way, a physical filter is connected to the telephone point in a house or office. The phone connection plugs into this filter along with the DSL modem.

The amount of data that can be sent on a DSL line depends on the technologies used, as well as service agreements with the DSL provider. The speed of the connection will also depend on the number of other people or devices using the connection at any one time.

DSL is divided into a range of connection types, each of which is intended to suit a specific audience. These include:

- Asymmetric Digital Subscriber Line (ADSL): provides a faster download speed than upload speed. This is the most popular form of DSL, used in homes and small organisations all over the world.

- Symmetric Digital Subscriber Line (SDSL): provides similar download and upload speeds. Some forms of SDSL do not carry analogue signals at all, preferring to use the whole cable to transmit digital information.

- High bit rate Digital Subscriber Line (HDSL): provides faster connection speeds using specific types of cable. HDSL is primarily used between telephone company exchanges, to develop the network infrastructure, rather than as a means to connect a user to the network.

ADSL

Asymmetric Digital Subscriber Line (ADSL) provides broadband with greater speed provided for downloading information rather than uploading.

ADSL is part of the DSL group of communication technologies and is probably the most common broadband connection used in homes and in small organisations. It is asymmetric, as the connection downloads data faster than it uploads it. For most users, this arrangement is suitable, as they will generally want to receive more Internet-based traffic than they will want to send.

Most users will only send information in the form of email, website searches and the use of websites for example, filling out forms or performing actions on a website. These activities do not require much bandwidth to perform. Viewing websites or multimedia smoothly requires greater bandwidth as more information needs to be sent from the website to the user.

ADSL speeds vary depending on line conditions, technology, distance from a local exchange and provider contracts. ADSL technology is also still developing, which means faster speeds are offered every few years.

Modem

A modem is a network device that allows data to be sent over the telephone lines.

The term modem is short for modulator/demodulator, which describes what the device does.

Computers store and read data digitally, but information is sent across telephone cables in waves. A modem modulates data to turn it into a wave that can be carried across the telephone network. This wave is then sent across the telephone network, where the receiving modem will demodulate the signal, translating the wave back into digital information.

At slow rates modem speeds are measured in baud rates. Baud rate is the speed at which a transmission signal between two communications devices changes every second. At very high rates modem speeds are measured in bits per second (bps).

The modem you need to send and receive information over the telephone network will depend on the type of connection you have. Some of the different kinds of modem include:

- Dialup modems: these are considered slow and becoming obsolete as broadband becomes more widely available.

- ADSL modems: are very common, and are used to connect to an ADSL broadband service.

- Optical modems: are used to connect to fibre optic networks. These are generally only used by large organisations with high speed connection requirements.

- Radio modems: used to transmit information over wireless connections.

- Cable modems: transmit information over RF television channels and are used where broadband is supplied over a cable connection.

Client server network architecture

'Client-server' architecture describes how computers, and some applications work with each other. The client will request information from the server, which stores and provides information, then the client can then process information and send it back to the server to store.

Network client

A network client is a computer or other device on the network that requests, receives and uses information from a network server.

The network client is a computer that a person works on. The server holds information, software or other resources that the client uses.

Network server

> A network server stores information and applications that can be used by clients connected to it.

A server can be an application or a piece of hardware. On most networks, the server is similar to a standard computer, but runs a specific server OS and generally contains a faster CPU and more storage.

Servers are used for a range of purposes, including:

- Managing network resources, such as printers.

- Providing centralised storage for files and information.

- Providing a central database to store information for different applications.

- Providing applications used by network clients.

A typical example of a client server architecture in operation can be found in call centres. Often, workers in call centres will use an application to take details or provide information to callers. The worker interacts with the application on their own computer.

However, the application itself, as well as the information it retrieves and stores is actually run from the server. This allows other workers in the same call centre to use the same application on their own computer to store and retrieve the same information. It also allows for quick recovery if a client computer breaks down suddenly, as information is constantly being written back to the server, rather than being held on specific computers.

The Internet and the web

Introduction

> The Internet is a 'network of networks', allowing any computer connected to it to communicate with any other connected computers.

The terms 'Internet' and 'World Wide Web' (or 'web') are often used interchangeably. However, they are different concepts.

The Internet is the collection of hardware, infrastructure, software, and protocols that allow communication between computers and networks.

Hardware includes servers, computers, and other network devices that store, process and serve information. The infrastructure refers to the cabling and connections that make this global communication physically possible. Software includes a range of applications used to develop, send, receive and display information. Protocols are rules that define how information, when it is disseminated over the internet, is sent, received and checked for errors. TCP / IP is the name given to the range of protocols used by the Internet. TCP / IP stands for Transmission Control Protocol / Internet Protocol. While only TCP and IP are explicitly named, TCP / IP generally refers to a suite of protocols used by computers and other devices to communicate over the Internet.

There are many types of communication that occur over the Internet, and the Web is just one of them. Other types of communication include email, file sharing, collaboration, remote access, streaming media and multimedia and Voice over Internet Protocol (VoIP). This list is not necessarily exhaustive as new technologies and applications are defined all the time.

The Web is a collection of interlinked pages and resources that are accessed via the Internet. It is used to communicate, publish and access information stored on servers in the Internet.

The Web uses a protocol called Hyper Text Transfer Protocol (HTTP) to communicate information. This is read by Internet browsers for example, Internet Explorer or Firefox and display for users. The Web consists of websites, which are web pages and other resources that can be accessed using the HTTP language. A range of media can be published on a web page, including text, graphics, audio, video and animations. Web pages and websites are navigated by clicking on hyperlinks that will call up and display another web page.

Internet versus Intranet

> An Intranet is a private network built using Internet technologies, but providing restricted access to unauthorised people.

An Intranet can be connected to the Internet, but restricts access to unauthorised persons by password protection or using a firewall that will prevent people outside an organisation's network from accessing it. Other than restricting access, an Intranet will act in exactly the same way as the Internet, as it is based on the same protocols and technologies.

Intranets are typically used to share or provide access to information within an organisation. Their development has helped to improve communication and collaboration among people as they are simple to understand, navigate and use.

Internet Protocol (IP) address

> (IP) is part of the transmission control protocol suite for the Internet, and helps regulate and run Internet communications based on accepted standards.

Every computer or device that communicates over a network using TCP / IP is assigned an IP address. This uniquely identifies the device on the network. The IP address is then used in communication to let other devices know where to send information for a computer. On a local or an organisation's network, IP addresses can be assigned randomly, as long as they are unique.

When connecting a private network to the Internet, a registered IP address must be used. This is known as an Internet address. This prevents addresses being duplicated across the Internet, which would disrupt communications, as no one could be sure where to send information.

Any device on the Internet can be uniquely identified with its IP address by tracking back from the registered IP address of the network that connects it to the Internet.

An IP address is a 32 bit string of binary code that identifies a network and host. To make them easier to understand and remember, IP addresses are normally displayed as a series of four blocks of decimal numbers. These can range from (0-255) separated by full stops. For example, the binary IP address:

10101000.11010100.11100010.11001100 is represented in decimal figures as 168.212.226.204

From the network's point of view, an IP address has two separate parts: the first part identifies a network and the second a host on that network. This division allows IP addresses to be assigned into classes. Each class defines which part of the IP address refers to a network, and which part refers to the host. The three classes of IP address are:

- Class A: which start with a binary 0 and use the first eight bits of the binary address to define the network. In decimal terms, the IP addresses range from 1.0.0.1 to 126.255.255.254. These addresses define 16 million hosts on each of the 127 networks. An example of this is 102.168.212.226. In this example, 102 identifies the network and 168.212.226 refers to the host.

- Class B: which start with a binary 10 and use the first 16 bits of the binary address to define the network. In decimal terms, the IP addresses range from 128.1.0.1 to 191.255.255.254. These addresses define 65,000 hosts on each of 16,000 networks. An example of this is 168.212.226.224. In this example, 168.212 identifies the network and 226.224 refers to the host.

- Class C: which start with a binary 110 and use the first 24 bits to define the network. In decimal terms, the IP addresses range from 192.0.1.1 to 223.255.254.254. These addresses define 254 hosts on each of 2 million networks. An example of this is 200.168.212.226. In this example, 200.168.212 identifies the network and 226 refers to the host.

Addresses are assigned by four regional agencies worldwide. These are:

- American Registry for Internet Numbers (ARIN): which administers IP addresses in North America, some of the Caribbean and sub-Saharan Africa.

- Réseaux IP Européens Network Coordination Centre (RIPE NCC): which administers addresses for Europe, the Middle East and parts of Africa and Asia.

- Latin American and Caribbean Internet Addresses Registry (LACNIC): which administers addresses for Latin America and the Caribbean.

- Asia Pacific Network Information Centre (APNIC): which administers addresses for the Asia Pacific region.

IP addresses are currently defined by the IPv4 standard. However, the number of unique addresses available is running out. A new standard IPv6 is in development to deal with the rapidly growing need for IP addresses.

Uniform Resource Locator (URL)

> A Uniform Resource Locator (URL) identifies where a file is on the web and how it can be retrieved.

A URL web address has two distinct parts:

- The first part identifies the scheme name or protocol that should be used to connect to the resource, for example, ftp or http.

- The second part provides a path to the location of the resource for example, adomain.com/folder/actualresource.html.

The protocol used will define how the second part of the address is formatted. Typically, a colon and two forward slashes is used to separate the protocol from the location.

The protocol will often define the application used to download a resource. File Transfer Protocol (FTP) will try to download files. This protocol also allows you to upload files, but to do this generally requires an FTP client application. HTTP requires an Internet browser to allow a web page to be displayed.

To provide an example:

ftp://example.com/firstfolder/secondfolder/actualresource.html will use File Transfer Protocol (FTP) to connect to the resource. FTP will download (if it can) the resource it finds at this address. Usually, FTP access is password protected to prevent unauthorised uploads.

http://example.com/firstfolder/secondfolder/actualresource.html will use HTTP to connect. HTTP will display (if it can) the resource it finds at this address.

Domain Name System (DNS)

> The Domain Name System (DNS) translates text names that users can recognise 'www.example.com' into IP addresses, 208.77.188.166', so Internet computers and devices can find a specific website. For this reason DNS is often referred to as the phone book of the Internet.

A domain is a distinct space on the Internet with shared IP and reflecting a person, group or an organisation through webpages.

The DNS allows websites to have names that are instantly recognisable and usable to people, instead of using IP addresses to send and receive information.

Domains have two parts: the domain name and a suffix. In our example, the domain name is 'example' and the suffix is '.com'. The domain name + suffix makes up the complete domain. www.example.com is not necessarily owned by the same person, group or organisation as www.example.org.

The suffix had originally been intended to denote a specific type of organisation. While a range of suffixes are available, the best known are probably:

- '.com', which is intended to denote a commercial business.

- '.org', which is intended to denote a charitable organisation.

In addition to these, there are suffixes for almost every country in the world. In practice, suffixes are not always used in this way. The name recognition of '.com' has meant many organisations will use this suffix with their own name as a domain.

Like IP addresses, domains must have a unique name, so that computers or devices sending and receiving information can be found quickly.

An organisation known as the Internet Corporation for Assigned Names and Numbers (ICANN) has ultimate responsibility for administering domains. They accredit domain name registrars around the world to manage domain names. These organisations have the authority to match an unused domain (or a domain within their control) to a specific IP address. They also operate name servers, which identify the IP address for domains. The information stored in these name servers is distributed throughout the Internet using a protocol known as 'whois'. In this way, devices on the Internet will know where to find or send information when communicating with another computer or device.

Firewalls

A firewall protects your network or computer from unauthorised access and prevents certain types of actions being performed. They can be implemented as software, hardware or a combination of both.

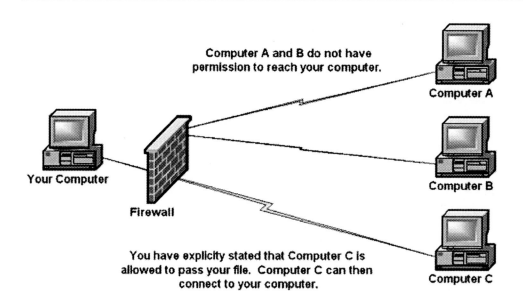

Any network, computer or other equipment that has access to the Internet should be protected by a firewall.

They work by checking all incoming and outbound communication against set criteria to decide whether to block or allow the information to pass.

Firewalls work in a variety of ways. Some of the most common are:

- Packet filters: which examine each packet, or piece of information being sent into and out of the network.

- Application gateways: which monitor the communication of specific applications.

- Proxy servers: which intercept all messages being sent into and out of the network. These will check the messages against set rules, but can also hide the true IP address of computers and devices within the network.

You can define the criteria that the firewall should check for. Generally, a firewall will prevent communication where:

- It includes a type of file that is considered dangerous.

- It does not trust the sender or intended recipient.

- The method of communication is suspicious (this can include very large messages sent over the network, emails with large attachments, but no message, etc).

When you install or control a firewall, it is important to ensure it is configured properly. You want it to block unwanted traffic, but allow valid traffic to pass through it.

Quite often, a firewall will block almost all communication, except Internet access, email communication and other vital network communications. You will need to create an exceptions list. This will tell the firewall that certain file types or addresses can be trusted, so it will allow communication through.

You also need to create a black list or blocked list. This identifies specific communications that should be blocked. Typical examples of this include blocking specific websites or certain file types, like MP3s from being sent over the network.

If you are installing a firewall:

- Read the documentation carefully.

- Make up a list of all the traffic you will need to block and/or allow.

- Set up the firewall during a quiet period so that disruption can be minimised and the firewall can be tested.

Importantly, firewalls also have logging and repositioning features to help manage and monitor security.

Common protocols

A protocol is a set of rules that define how two devices connect, communicate, and transfer data between them.

TCP / IP

TCP / IP is fundamental to Internet communication. When the term TCP / IP is used, it refers to a whole suite of protocols including FTP, SMTP among others.

TCP / IP is composed of four layers, each of which uses one or more protocols to perform specific tasks:

- Link layer: is used to physically connect a computer or node to a network. This layer is responsible for preparing data for transmission by breaking it into pieces known as 'packets'. This is similar to placing a letter in an envelope so that it can be carried through a postal system.

- Internet layer: is used to address the packets prepared by the link layer across a network (or the Internet). This is like posting your letter, so the postman can pick it up, identify the end address and decide where best to post it to. The IP protocol is used at this layer.

- Transport layer: is used to set up a connection between computers and transfer data between them. This is like the post office deciding the best way to get your letter to the intended recipient. It may need to be driven to another city, or even flown to another country. The TCP protocol is used at this layer.

- Application layer: defines the protocols that applications use to communicate and allows applications to use the other layers to communicate information This is like your recipient opening the envelope and reading your letter. They may use the information in it, or decide to reply to you. Their action will depend on the content of your letter. Familiar applications, such as HTTP (which handles websites), SMTP (which handles email), and FTP (which handles file transfer) work at this level.

TCP / IP uses a client/server network architecture, where the client computer will request information from the server. The server provides the information and the client can save, or process the information. In most cases, the client cannot rewrite or change the information stored on the server. However, the client computer can modify the information and save it to its own hard drive.

HTTP

> Hyper Text Transfer Protocol (HTTP) is the protocol used to define how websites look and act.

When you type a URL into an Internet browser, this sends an HTTP command to the device that is connecting you to the Internet. The device seeks the address you have entered and directs the computer to that address.

When your computer is communicating with the server at the address you entered, data is transferred to your computer over TCP / IP. This data is then deciphered and displayed by HTTP through your Internet browser.

Clicking on links or performing other actions send further HTTP commands to the server that will be executed on your computer for example, opening a new web page, or submitting information to a website.

HTTPS

> Hyper Text Transfer Protocol (HTTPs) is used to send or receive information securely over the Internet.

The HTTPS protocol is used when websites request personal, private or sensitive information. An example of this is an ecommerce website that requests credit card details to facilitate payment.

HTTPS applies encryption and a security certificate, known as a Secure Socket Layer (SSL) certificate to the data sent and received by a website.

This prevents unauthorised people from intercepting or reading the information being sent through the Internet. Some indications that you are connected to a website using HTTPS include:

- "https://" being displayed at the start of the URL in the address bar.

- In some browsers, the address bar is highlighted in yellow.

- A padlock icon is displayed at the bottom right corner of the browser window.

FTP

> File Transfer Protocol (FTP) is used to transfer larger files across the Internet.

While HTTP and SMTP can be used to send and receive files, they have file size limits, and they do not work as well when file sizes becomes larger than 2-3MB.

For these larger files, FTP allows you to upload and download files from a specific location.

FTP connections are typically password protected. The files transferred by FTP include applications, large images, video or other media. Sometimes, FTP is used to provide a complete folder of individual documents or other files. This saves time and energy, as you don't need to send documents individually. Instead, you can store them to a folder and provide the address (and login details) to the other person, who can then download the files.

IPX / SPX

> Internetwork Packet Exchange / Sequenced Packet Exchange (IPX / SPX) is a protocol owned by Novell that transfers data between Novell NetWare clients and servers.

The IPX / SPX protocol was historically used in local networks and internetworks. It operates in the same way as the TCP / IP suite, providing a method for computers and devices to communicate over the network.

However, the ubiquity of TCP / IP has meant that IPX / SPX is used less often, and generally only within private networks.

Quick Quiz

Select the correct answer from the following multiple-choice questions:

1. Which type of network would be most suitable for an organisation with offices in two countries?

    a   LAN

    b   WAN

    c   CAN

    d   MAN

2. Which method of connection uses short-range radio technology?

    a   SCSI

    b   Coaxial

    c   USB

    d   Bluetooth

3. A network belonging to a particular organisation based on TCP / IP protocols is otherwise known as:

    q   Internet

    b   Intranet

    c   Web

    d   Server

4. Class C binary addresses start with:

    a   0

    b   1

    c   100

    d   110

5. Which firewall technique intercepts all messages entering and leaving the network?

    a   Packet Switch

    b   Application gateway

    c   Proxy server

    d   Telnet server

Answers to Quick Quiz

1   b   WAN

2   d   Bluetooth

3   b   Internet

4   d   110

5   c   Proxy server

Operating system

Concepts

Connect

Operating System

Install

Admin

Measuring points

▸ Recognise the most common operating systems
▸ Know different ways to install an operating system: by downloading from the Internet, from a network, installing from a CD
▸ Recognise a file or directory system is an operational platform for a network
▸ Know how to install, upgrade an operating system
▸ Know how to create a start up disk
▸ Use a GUI to map drives, create shortcuts and manage desktop icons
▸ Set up a VPN client
▸ Set up desktop configuration with different themes, backgrounds, taskbar orientations etc
▸ Recognise different file types: application files, temporary files, system files etc and know where they might be stored

▸ Understand what the boot menu is
▸ Understand how to partition a hard drive
▸ View available hardware and its configuration
▸ Start the computer in safe mode
▸ Monitor server performance
▸ Obtain the IP address for a computer (i.e. PING a server)
▸ Use network software to monitor network, hardware, software performance, memory usage rates
▸ Monitor and analyse system events log
▸ Know the purpose of backing up
▸ Know how to schedule a backup, restore backup
▸ Know how to check (verify) a backup
▸ Know different media types for backing up, know about rotational backup schemes, and the importance of offsite backups
▸ Know the meaning of the term surge protector
▸ Understand UPS and what it is used for

Introduction

Operating systems are the software platform for computers and networks. This chapter covers common operating systems and how they are used to run and manage computing systems. Installation, configuration and administration of operating systems and performance covered.

Common operating systems

The Operating System (OS), also known as a platform, is a piece of software that controls the computer.

The operating system manages the computers resources and allows the applications software to run, for example Microsoft Word and Internet Explorer, etc.

The most widely distributed types of operating system have been developed by Microsoft. Each type of Windows platform (2000, XP, Vista) is a different type of operating system, and so manages the computer's resources in different ways.

Other popular operating system developers are:

- Apple: which uses its own operating system to manage its computers and hardware.

- Linux: an open source platform that can be used to manage computers.

- Novell: a proprietary operating system used in large scale installations.

All of these operating systems are GUI-based. GUI stands for Graphical User Interface, and as the name suggests, refers to the fact that you make commands for the operating systems to execute through a graphical interface. This could be double-clicking to open a folder, or run a file.

Other operating systems, like IBM's OS/2 and Microsoft's DOS, can still be used though generally by specialists.

These platforms do not use a GUI, so to use them, you have to type in specific commands that the computer can understand and perform.

As identified earlier, the tasks an operating performs include:

- Recognising and processing inputs, for example, keystrokes on a keyboard.

- Processing user data and outputting it appropriately (for example, displaying information on a screen).

- Running (or executing) applications.

- Ensuring all applications have enough resources to run efficiently.

- Managing file systems and data storage.

- Ensuring hardware added to the computer is recognized.

- Maintaining security on the computer.

- Networking with other computers and/or servers.

Installing an operating system

In this section installing an operating system on a computer is explained. Most computers are delivered with operating system discs, or with the operating system already installed. However, you may want to use a different operating system, or upgrade the operating system running on older computers.

In a network, the operating system will determine how different devices communicate and share information with each other, allowing users to share files, folders or directories, for example, within a Quality Management System (QMS) on their computers, as well as on a network server or drive.

It is good practice to run the same operating system on all computers using the network, and also to ensure the operating system running on the server is compatible with this to ensure and maintain information security across the network.

There are various ways to install or upgrade an operating system. It can be done directly from the installation CD's that come with the computer. You can also perform a network installation, which is an efficient way of installing or upgrading an operating system for multiple computers across the organisation. Also it is now quite common for software developers to offer the latest version of their operating systems for download from their websites.

Back up all data

The operating system controls how data is stored, made available and used on any computer.

As such it is an important piece of infrastructure for the organisation. Even the simplest organisational directory system, with its files, folders and records, needs to be there to ensure the organisation can do its work.

Before installing an operating system, you should create backups of any information that is currently on the computer. Remember, the operating system controls the computer, so if you have any problems during installation, or when the operating system is running, you could lose valuable information. Backing up the data will ensure you have a copy of it, should you run into trouble.

Creating backups is dealt with in more detail later on in this chapter.

Identify hardware and software requirements

The computer vendor ensures that the operating system delivered works with the computer. However, if you are using a different operating system or performing an upgrade, you need to make sure the operating system can work with the different hardware and software on the computer.

For Windows XP and Vista, you can check whether your computer's hardware and software will be compatible with the operating system using Microsoft's Upgrade Adviser application. For Windows Vista, you can visit their website to access the Upgrade Adviser:

http://www.microsoft.com/windows/windows-vista/get/upgrade-advisor.aspx

The Upgrade Adviser scans your computer and provides a report to let you know of any potential problems and how they can be resolved.

For Windows XP, you can click the *Check System Compatibility* link which is displayed when you insert the Windows XP CD into your CD drive.

Alternatively, you can view Microsoft's *Hardware Compatibility List*. This is available online at:

http://www.microsoft.com/whdc/hcl/default.aspx

If your hardware is not compatible with the operating system, it is best to seek advice as to what to do next. Sometimes, you can still install the operating system, but will need to also install drivers for the hardware. In other cases, the advice may be to replace the hardware, especially if it is older.

Decide whether to perform a clean install or an upgrade

A clean install means removing all existing data on the computer, repartitioning and reformatting your hard drive, and then installing your operating system. This is generally required where you are installing a new operating system (as opposed to just upgrading to a newer version of the same operating system), or if the computer is corrupted for example, by a virus or other problem that is preventing the computer from working properly.

An upgrade means replacing an older version of the operating system with a newer one. You may want to do this to ensure all computers in your organisation are running on the same system. Running the same platform means you can buy software for computers in your organisation and be sure that the same software version will be compatible with all computers.

Clean install

To perform a clean install, you will need to boot, (or start up), your computer from the installation CD. The concept of 'booting up' is dealt with in more detail later. In most cases, when you put the CD in the drive, you will be told specifically how to do this. If this does not occur, you will need to set the computer's BIOS to allow booting from CD. How you set the BIOS to allow the computer to boot from CD will depend on the manufacturer. You should consult your computer's manual for more instructions. If your computer will not allow you to boot from the CD, you will need to create a setup disk. This is dealt with in more detail in the next section.

Use the following steps to perform a standard installation of an operating system on a computer:

> ### Actions
>
> ▶ 1. Insert the installation CD into the CD drive and restart your computer.
>
> ▶ 2. When prompted, follow the on-screen instructions. Alternatively, the computer may tell you it is automatically booting from the CD.
>
> ▶ 3. At the *Welcome to Setup* screen, press *Enter*.
>
> ▶ 4. Read the *licence terms and conditions*. Then press the *F8* key to agree to them and continue.
>
> ▶ 5. Follow the instructions to select and format the physical space on the drive, where you want to install the operating system.
>
> ▶ 6. Follow the instructions to install the operating system.

You can partition a drive to allow for multiple platform installations.

After the installation process, you will be asked to activate the operating system. You usually can do this over the Internet or by phoning the customer service of your operating system supplier. You do not have to activate the product straight away, but reminders will display on startup to encourage you to do this.

To activate the operating system over the Internet, enable the *Yes, let's activate Windows over the Internet now* option on the activation screen. The rest of this process is automatic. You should use this option where you are activating an operating system on multiple computers, as it will save time.

To activate the operating system over the phone, enable the Yes, *I want to telephone a customer service representative to activate Windows* option, and then follow the instructions provided.

Upgrade

You may want to upgrade your operating system so that the computer is running on a similar system to the other computers in your network. Operating system suppliers regularly release new software versions which provide enhanced features and security. It is good practice to keep operating systems up-to-date.

To upgrade the operating system from a CD, follow these steps:

Actions

▶ 1. Insert the installation CD into the CD drive.

▶ 2. This should start the installation, click *Install Windows*.

    a. If the CD does not run automatically, select *Start* click *Run*.

    b. Type CD drive letter (may be D, E or F) followed by \:setup.exe

    c. Click *OK*.

▶ 3. Select *Upgrade* from the *Installation Type* drop down list.

▶ 4. Click *Next*.

▶ 5. Follow the instructions provided.

You can also upgrade the operating system version over the internet.

Installing on a network

For large organisations, where there may be many machines on different networks, it would not be efficient to do an individual installation of an operating system onto each machine. An efficient option is to save the operating system software to a shared folder of a network drive, and then perform installations from the network drive.

In medium to large organisations more advanced installation methods are employed, especially when many identical computers need to be configured.

A common method is to place the source file in a shared directory on a network server. Then, whenever you need to install a new operating system, it is a simple task of booting up the computer, connecting to the source application on the network and starting the installation from there. This method has many variations.

Image installation

Another type of installation that is very popular for recreating standard configurations is an image installation.

An image is a complete copy of a hard disk volume on which an operating system and usually all required application software have been pre-installed.

Images can be placed on CD media, in which case technical support runs special software on the computer that copies the image onto the local hard drives.

In some organisations it is important to have a standard configuration and installation for operating system and applications software. Image installations take a copy of the standard hard disk installation required, and then with special software copy an exact replica of this installation onto other computers.

Creating startup disks

> Startup disks are specially prepared to allow installation of an operating system from a digital storage medium, for example from a CD, DVD, or flash drive.

With Microsoft, startup disks are used to perform a clean installation of an operating system when the original operating system CD has been lost or damaged, or will not start up or 'boot' from the CD drive.

> In computing terms, booting up (bootstrapping) is a series of processes the computer runs in order to start working. These processes include identifying the hardware configuration and launching the operating system.

Historically, startup disks were prepared using several floppy disks although this is uncommon nowadays.

To create Windows XP setup disks

If your computer can 'boot' from the CD drive or through the network, it is good practice to use one of these methods to install the operating system, to provide for recovery from operating system failure or corruption. Microsoft does not support the creation of startup disks on products developed after Windows Vista. Windows Millenium and XP both allow for startup disk creation.

Creating and using startup disks will only work for you if:

- You are creating a new clean installation from a Windows CD.

- Your CD drive is working,

Use the following steps to create a Windows XP startup disk:

> **Actions**
>
> ▶ 1. Download the Windows XP setup disk that matches the installation CD you have from the Microsoft website.
>
> ▶ 2. Double-click on the file you downloaded to run and prepare the setup disk.
>
> ▶ 3. Follow the instructions provided to copy the setup files to the boot device.

Booting up

Once you have created your setup disks, use the following steps to install Windows:

> **Actions**
>
> ▶ 1. Insert the setup disk in CD drive.
>
> ▶ 2. Start or restart your computer.
>
> ▶ 3. You may be prompted to press a key to boot from the drive, or the computer will tell you it is booting from the drive.
>
> ▶ 4. Follow the instructions to begin the installation process.
>
> ▶ 5. You will need to use the operating system CD to complete installation.

Booting from Windows (XP, Vista) CD/DVDs will allow you to not only install / re-install Windows but will also allow you to troubleshoot the system.

This CD also contains *Startup Repair*, which you can use to repair Windows if a problem prevents it from starting correctly. *Startup Repair* can automatically fix many of the problems that in the past required a boot disk to fix.

The boot menu

> A boot menu triggers a sequence of actions for the computer, and selects which drives or devices to read from first as the computer attempts to start up. The boot device then loads the operating system onto the computer.

The boot menu is generally only used where a problem has occurred, or where operating system installation or repair is being performed.

Boot menu options also allow you to:

- Restrict the number of features that the computer platform loads, which is used when a bad system crash has occurred and the computer has become unstable.

- Tell the computer where to look to find the operating system to load, which is used when installing a new operating system, or running system tools on a computer whose operating system has become corrupted.

Boot devices

Typical boot devices include a computer's hard drive and its CD/DVD drive. There are also boot chips, which are used to load an operating system from a network server.

Any device that is recognised by the computer's BIOS can be a boot device. This includes external devices connected by SCSI or USB, or even a floppy drive (although these are less common now).

When a computer starts up, its BIOS will look for known boot devices to load the operating system. The BIOS can be configured to look for the operating system on several devices in a specified order. The BIOS will load the operating system from the first device that holds it.

To give an example, the BIOS may be configured to look for the operating system in the following way:

- CD/DVD Drive

- The computer's hard drive

- A network location

In this example, when the computer starts up, the BIOS will first check the CD/DVD drive to see if it has an operating system. If it does, the operating system will load from here. If it does not, the BIOS will check the computer's hard drive. If it cannot find an operating system here, it will check a specified network location.

Desktop configuration

A GUI (or Graphical User Interface) is the term used to describe the way users interact with the computer using visual icon scheme. Files, folders are all represented visually to make it easier and more efficient to use the computer.

With a GUI, the desktop, or the visualisation of a work space, is the starting point for users to interact with the computer.

You can configure the desktop to make it easier for the user to find information and use the computer. The options available range from changing the wallpaper (or background) on the desktop to creating shortcuts to specific files and arranging them in a way that makes sense to you. In this section, different desktop configuration options are dealt with.

The desktop background also known as wallpaper can be an image from a personal collection or one that comes pre-installed with Windows.

Set the desktop background

To change a desktop background, you need to access the display options from the control panel and select an image on your computer to display. You can also set different themes, which define the colours of text and images on your computer.

Use the following steps to access and modify various display options on a computer:

Actions

▶ 1. Click *Start*, select *Control Panel*.

▶ 2. Click *Display*.

Actions

▶ 3. In the *Display Properties* dialogue box, click the *Desktop* tab.

▶ 4. Click on one of the *Background* images listed to view a preview of it.

▶ 5. Click *Browse* to select a picture stored on the computer.

▶ 6. Click *OK* to apply the selected picture as the desktop background.

Set different themes

Actions

▶ 1. In the *Display Properties* dialogue box, click *Themes*.

▶ 2. Select a theme from the list to view a preview of it.

▶ 3. Click *OK* to apply the chosen theme.

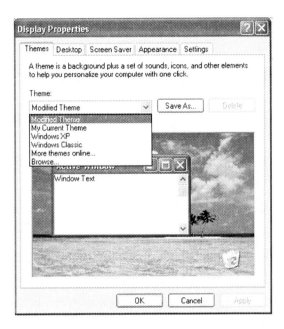

 With Vista, the same functionality can be applied by selecting *Start*, clicking *Control Panel* and selecting *Personalization,* or by right-clicking on the *Desktop* and selecting *Personalization*.

Taskbar orientation

You can move the taskbar so that it sits along the bottom, top, left or right edge of the screen. It can also be hidden, so that applications that are running are given more screen space. To make it easier to access applications that are frequently used, you can also add shortcuts to applications.

Use the following steps to personalise a taskbar:

Actions

▶ 1. Click *Start*, select *Control Panel*.

▶ 2. Double-click *Taskbar and Start menu*.

The *Taskbar and Start Menu Properties* dialogue box will display.

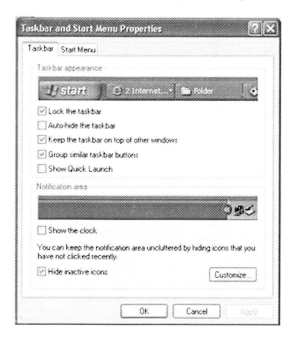

Configuration options available are:

- Lock the taskbar

- Auto-hide the taskbar

- Keep taskbar on top of other windows

- Group similar taskbar buttons

- Show *Quick Launch* for applications

- Show the clock

- Hide inactive icons

Creating shortcuts

Shortcuts are links to files, folders or applications that are used regularly. A shortcut can be placed on a desktop to let a user quickly perform regular tasks without having to repeat selections and clicks.

There are two ways to add a shortcut to a desktop:

- Create it from the *Start* menu.
- Create it by selecting the item in a folder.

Use the following steps to create a shortcut from the *Start* menu.

Actions

▷ 1. Select *Start*, and click *Explore*.

▷ 2. Locate the folder, file, or program in the *Folders* directory, and then click the item to open it.

▷ 3. Click on the icon representing the item.

▷ 4. Click *File* on the toolbar, and then *Create Shortcut* on the drop-down menu that appears.

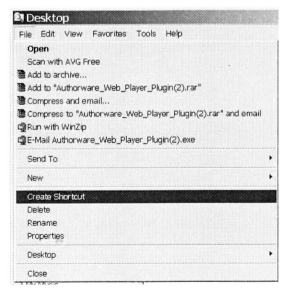

Alternatively, you can create a shortcut from the folder where the item you want to link to is stored. Use the following steps to do this:

Actions

▷ 1. Navigate to the item that you want to create a shortcut for.

▷ 2. Right-click on the item.

▷ 3. Click *Send To* and select *Desktop (create shortcut)*.

Managing desktop icons

You can drag icons around the desktop. This allows you to place icons in locations that make them easier and more intuitive to use. To move an icon, click on it, and drag it to the desired location.

You can also arrange icons and align them to a grid. This grid is invisible, but will align icons in orderly rows and columns.

Actions

▶ 1. Right-click on the desktop.

▶ 2. Click *Arrange Icons By* and select *Align to Grid*.

If you just want to arrange icons into neat columns and rows, you can get Windows to Auto Arrange them. Doing this will bring all the icons together and arrange them into columns.

Use the following steps to Auto Arrange the icons:

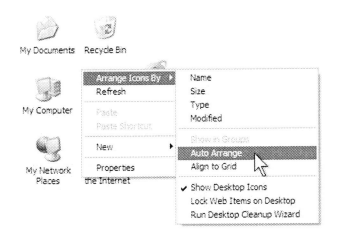

In Windows Vista, you can right-click on the desktop and select *Sort By* to arrange icons by:

- *Name*, alphabetically.

- *Size*, orders icons according to how big they are.

- *Type*, groups files of the same type together.

- *Modified*, orders icons according to how recently they have been used. All of these desktop confirmation points are often set up in advance to help users work more productively.

Administering hard drives and network drives

Introduction

Managing the drives on your organisation's computers and network will help you to organise the information your organisation stores in such a way that it will be easy to locate and share with others. This will help users to collaborate and improve productivity. In this section, some of the strategies you can employ to administer your drives effectively are covered.

Partitioning a hard drive

Partitioning a hard drive divides the drive into sections. You can then store specific information or even install a different operating system, in each partition.

Windows XP

Partitioning a hard drive makes the information stored on it easier to manage. It can also allow you to run multiple operating systems on a computer. However, it is typically used to separate storage space for the computer's operating system, applications and actual file storage. This makes backing up the drive easier.

To partition a drive, your computer will remove all existing partitions. This can cause data loss and possibly create problems for the operating system. As much as possible you should partition a drive when it is new. If there is information on the drive, make sure you create a backup before creating the partitions. This will help you retrieve any information that could be lost during the partitioning process.

Before partitioning a drive, you need to consider:

- What you will use each partition for?

- What type of file system will suit this use (FAT32 or NTFS)?

- How much space will be required in each partition?

FAT files

FAT (File Allocation Table) files are file systems which allow for partitioning of drives. File names can have up to 11 characters with DOS operating systems and 255 characters for later versions of Windows operating systems such as Windows '95.

FAT 32 is a 32 bit file allocation table system. Developed for Windows '95 service release 2 and later versions, it provides for a single partition volume size of up to 2 TB's (terabytes).

NTFS is the Windows NT file system. NTFS supports file names of up to 256 characters. NTFS has additional security features and supports multi-volume partitions in the drive of up to 16 exabytes (1 billion gigabytes).

With Windows XP, you can partition your drive when installing the operating system. You can also use the operating system installation CD to create a partition after the operating system has been installed.

To partition a disk using the Windows XP Setup disk, you need to access the list of partitions using the Setup utility, then define a new partition. The following actions assume that Windows XP is already installed on the computer. If this is not the case, you should follow the instructions for installing the operating system, and partition the drive during that process.

Use the following steps to access the partitions list:

Actions

▶ 1. Insert the Windows XP installation CD into the CD/DVD drive.

▶ 2. Follow the standard instructions and if Windows XP is already installed, you will be prompted to repair it. Press the *Esc* button to bypass this.

▶ 3. This will allow you to access the partitions list in the Setup utility.

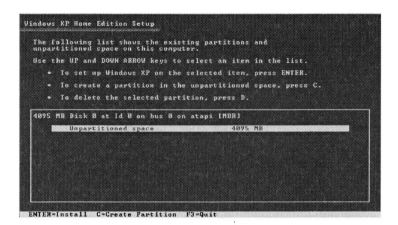

Once you have accessed the partitions list in the Setup utility, you can define a new partition. If you want to create a partition where one already exists, you will need to delete the existing partition before creating a new one. This will remove any data stored in the existing partition. You can partition any non partitioned section of the disk, once there is enough space to do so.

Use the following steps to create a new partition:

Actions

▶ 1. In the partitions list, use the arrow keys to select an non partitioned (or a partitioned) section of the drive to create your new partition in.

▶ 2. If you need to delete a partition:

    a. Highlight the partition.

    b. Press *D*.

    c. Press the *Enter* key.

    d. Press *L* to confirm deleting the partition.

▶ 3. Press *C* to create a new partition.

▶ 4. Type the size you want the partition to be (in MBs), or press *Enter* to use the maximum size available.

At this point, the Setup utility will ask whether you want to install Windows XP and to select a partition to do so. Press the *F3* key twice to exit this process and return to format your partition(s).

The following options can be used to format the partition:

- Format the partition by using the NTFS file system (Quick).

- Format the partition by using the FAT file system (Quick).

- Format the partition by using the NTFS file system.

- Format the partition by using the FAT file system.

- Leave the current file system intact (no changes).

```
Windows XP Home Edition Setup

   The partition you selected is not formatted. Setup will now
   format the partition.

   Use the UP and DOWN ARROW keys to select the file system
   you want, and then press ENTER.

   If you want to select a different partition for Windows XP,
   press ESC.

      Format the partition using the NTFS file system (Quick)
      Format the partition using the FAT file system (Quick)
      Format the partition using the NTFS file system
      Format the partition using the FAT file system

 ENTER=Continue   ESC=Cancel
```

Use the arrow keys to select the formatting option you want to use on your partition, then press *Enter*.

The formatting option you select should take into account:

- Whether you will want to transfer files between partitions on the computer and what formatting the other partitions have.

- Whether you will want to transfer files to a network backup/storage device and what formatting that device uses.

It is important that you use the same formatting system if you want to move files between partitions or onto other disks.

The Setup utility will format the drive partition. Once this is complete, follow the instructions to either:

- Repeat the process to create another partition.

- Exit the Setup utility.

Windows Vista

Windows Vista has built-in software to let you to create, format and resize drive partitions without having to use a specific Setup utility.

To partition and format a drive using Windows Vista, you need first to access the Microsoft Management Console. Then 'Shrink' the C Drive and use the extra space to create a new partition, and format it.

Use the following steps to access the Microsoft Management Console and view current disk partitions:

Actions

▶ 1. Click *Start*, select *Run*.

▶ 2. Enter 'mmc' in the *Open* field.

▶ 3. Click *OK* to open the *Microsoft Management Console*.

▶ 4. Click *Computer Management* in the right pane.

▶ 5. Click *Disk Management* in the right pane.

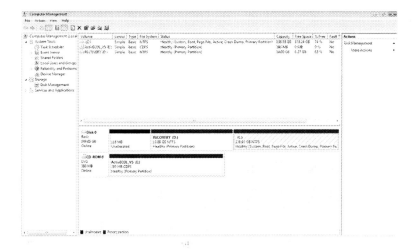

Use the following steps to shrink your C drive:

Actions

▶ 1. Right-click on the drive you want to partition.

▶ 2. Select *Shrink Volume*.

▶ 3. In the *Shrink C* dialogue box that opens, type or click the up and down arrows to specify the size you want to shrink the disk by. You might choose 20% – 30% or more.

▶ 4. Click *Shrink*.

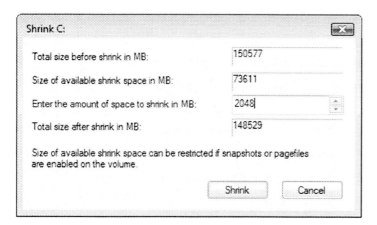

Use the following steps to use the new unallocated space to create a new partition.

Actions

▶ 1. In the *Microsoft Management Console*, right-click on the unallocated space.

▶ 2. Click *New Simple Volume*.

▶ 3. Format the new partition and provide a name for it.

The steps will create and format a new partition. You can view this partition by opening *My Computer* and viewing the drives on the computer.

You will also be able to store files to the new partition.

> **Actions**
>
> ▶ 1. Format the new partition as NTFS and give it a name.
>
> ▶ 2. Vista will format the newly-created partition inside the *Microsoft Management Console*.
>
> ▶ 3. Now the newly-created partition will be viewable in *My Computer* and available to read and write to.

Mapping a network drive

> Mapping a network drive means assigning a drive letter (such as D:, X:, or J:) to a shared disk drive.

Mapping network drives helps you share resources, as you can simply save or move files and folders to the network drive, which other users can also access.

Shared network drives are displayed in *My Computer* and *Windows Explorer* similarly to the drives on your own computer.

To create a network drive:

- Select a drive (or folder) to share and assign it as a shared resource.

- Label the resource.

- Make it available on the network.

To perform both these actions, you will need to be logged in as an administrator on the computer you are using.

Use the following steps to share a folder on a computer or server:

> **Actions**
>
> ▶ 1. Click *Start*, select *My Computer*.
>
> ▶ 2. You can either:
>
>   a. Click a drive to share everything in it.
>
>   b. Double-click a drive to locate a specific folder to share.
>
> ▶ 3. Right-click the drive or folder you want to share.
>
> ▶ 4. Click *Sharing and Security*.
>
> ▶ 5. Enable the *Share this folder on the network* option.

Once you have shared a folder or drive, you connect each computer to that folder so they can share it.

To map a drive or folder:

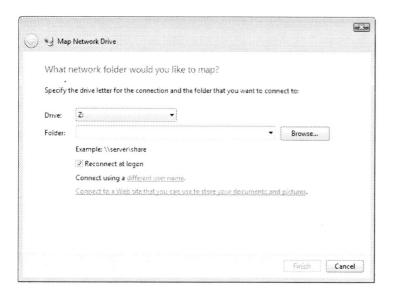

Setting up a VPN

A Virtual Private Network (VPN) allows users who are not in your physical offices to access files on the network. A VPN provides secure access to the network using an Internet connection.

To configure a VPN using Windows XP:

Actions

▶ 1. Click *Start*, and select *Control Panel*.

▶ 2. In *Control Panel*, double-click *Network Connections*.

▶ 3. In the *Network Tasks* pane on the left, click *Create a new connection*. This opens the *Network Connection Wizard*.

▶ 4. In the *Network Connection Wizard*, click *Next*.

▶ 5. Enable the *Connect to the network at my workplace* option, and click *Next*.

▶ 6. Enable the *Virtual Private Network connection* option, and click *Next*.

▶ 7. Provide a name for the connection. This is to make it easy to identify the VPN connection. As an example 'Work VPN' or the organisation's name could be used.

▶ 8. Select how you are connecting to the Internet. This could be using a dialup connection, or a dedicated connection, such as cable, DSL, etc. Then click *Next*.

▶ 9. Type the host name (for example, organisationdomain.com, or the IP address of the VPN server, which will allow access to your network. Then click *Next*.

▶ 10. Click *Finish* to exit.

The *Network Connection Wizard* will then test the connection and ensure you can connect to the VPN. A message will confirm that the connection has been successful.

File types

In computing, files are generally identified by being assigned a filename. The filename consists of a meaningful alphanumeric string and a filename extension. For example, 'payrollmasterHQ35.txt': payrollmasterHQ35 identifies the file and txt extension identifies the format of the file as a text file. This section explains how files are loosely categorised into file types and the use of filename extensions.

Temporary files

A temporary file is created by an application or operating system to store information while a file is being worked on or a process is in progress.

fsd_41eeca
770000.tmp

Temporary files are generally used to allow recovery copies of files to be made, should the computer crash suddenly. They are also used to store and retrieve information temporarily. These files have the file extension '.tmp'.

Temporary files are generally invisible to users, because they are usually deleted when a file is closed or a process ends. However, this is not always the case, and sometimes temporary files are kept even after an application has closed or a process ends. Over time, this can affect a computer's performance as memory is being used to store temporary files that could be used for other information.

Application files

> Application programs output files in various format. Any program that wants to process a file must know the format of the file it is trying to read to interpret the data. Currently, by convention, application files that you generally work with have filename extensions that allow programs in the same application area, word processing, spreadsheets, processing images/photos etc. to interpret files created by similar programs.

Application files are the files that you generally work with and use on a computer. Some examples of application files and their extensions include:

- The Word file extension is .doc

- The Excel file extension is .xls

- Web pages are often (but not always) .html

- The Photoshop file extension is .psd

Not all applications can reprocess a file stored in a file format they can read. For example, media players cannot modify MP3 files.

System files

> System files are used by the operating system to manage the computer. They are usually invisible to end users.

System files are used to provide information to the operating system and other programs. System files may also consist of executable code to run processes and perform other tasks that the user would generally not need to know about. However, these tasks are fundamental to the running of the computer and its operating system. You should not delete or try to alter these files in any way, for example any setup or initiation files; .sys, .ini etc.

Monitoring performance

Introduction

This section explains how some aspects of computer performance can be monitored so that remedial action can be taken. It covers the identification of all the parts of computer configuration, highlighting possible problem areas and poor connectivity. The approach to safe recovery is explained. It also discusses some of the management tools available to monitor processes and identify capacity constraints.

Viewing hardware devices

You can view a computer's hardware components using the *Windows Device Manager*. This is an applications tool that allows you to display and control hardware devices. Use the following steps to view hardware attached to your computer using the *Device Manager*:

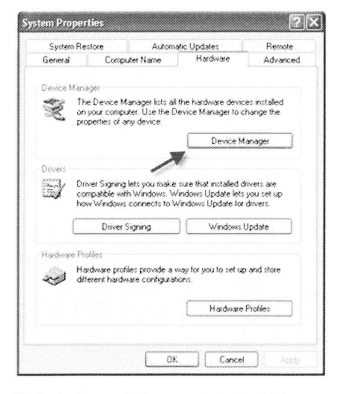

Actions

▶ 1. Click *Start*, select *Control Panel*.

▶ 2. Click *System*.

▶ 3. In the *Systems Properties* dialogue box, click *Hardware*.

▶ 4. Click *Device Manager*.

The *Device Manager* displays every device that Windows recognises organised in special groups called types.

All devices of the same type are grouped under the same type heading. Click on a + symbol to see all the devices of a particular type.

The *Device Manager* lists every piece of hardware connected to the computer. These are listed according to a category, for example printers, drives, keyboards, etc.

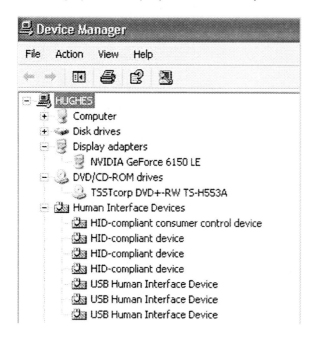

The *Device Manager* will let you know if there is a problem with a piece of hardware in the following ways:

• An exclamation mark (!) in a yellow triangle means the hardware is not functioning properly.

• A red X beside a piece of hardware means the device is disabled. Right-click on it to enable it.

• A list of 'Other devices' indicates there is hardware attached to the computer that Windows does not recognise.

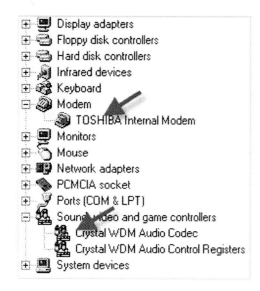

If a device is not listed here, but you know it is connected to the computer, there is probably a problem with the hardware itself.

To check a piece of hardware that is not working properly, right-click on it and select *Update Driver*. This will help you find the most recent driver for the part.

If this does not work, Windows can help you further troubleshoot the device. Right-click on it and select *Properties*. In the *Properties* dialogue box, click the *Troubleshoot* button to tag and do this.

Starting in safe mode

Performance

Modern computer systems provide a range of performance, analysis and monitoring tools that are used to maintain systems and ensure system platforms run efficiently.

> Safe mode is a recovery start mode which runs the computer with the minimum number of required processes.

Safe mode is used where some change in the computer has made it unstable. This could be a software or hardware change. By starting the computer in safe mode, you can make changes (or restore the computer to a safer configuration) in a more stable environment.

Safe mode is accessed in two ways:

- If a computer crashes in the middle of a process, it will offer to start in safe mode.

- You can force the computer to start in safe mode by selecting it as a boot option when the computer starts up.

There are different types of Safe Mode:

- *Safe Mode*: will load Windows using the minimum amount of processes required.

- *Safe Mode with Networking*: will load Windows with as few processes as possible, but include support for network or Internet access.

- *Safe Mode with Command Prompt*: loads safe mode but provides a command prompt interface with which you interact with the computer.

This section deals with how you start the first Safe Mode option. Begin by starting up the computer. Press *F8* when you see the screen offering advanced boot options. This is displayed for about 5-7 seconds. If you see the Windows XP splash page, you will need to try again.

After you press *F8*, the following screen should be displayed. Use the up and down arrows to select the type of Safe Mode you want to use and press *Enter* to continue:

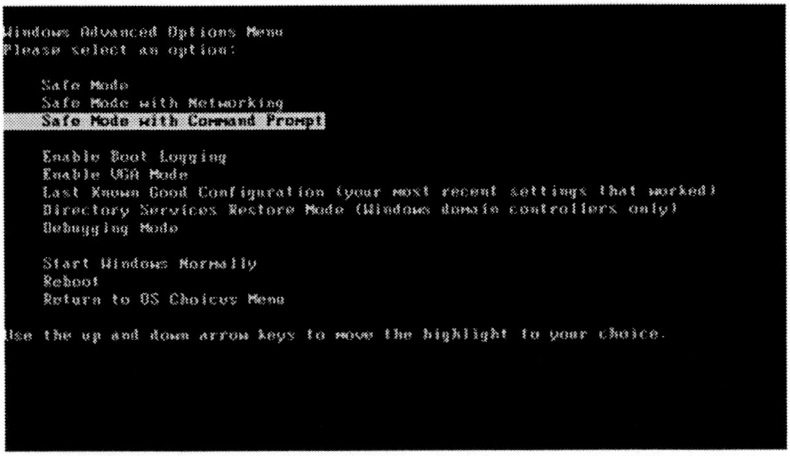

```
Windows Advanced Options Menu
Please select an option:

    Safe Mode
    Safe Mode with Networking
    Safe Mode with Command Prompt

    Enable Boot Logging
    Enable VGA Mode
    Last Known Good Configuration (your most recent settings that worked)
    Directory Services Restore Mode (Windows domain controllers only)
    Debugging Mode

    Start Windows Normally
    Reboot
    Return to OS Choices Menu

Use the up and down arrow keys to move the highlight to your choice.
```

The computer will display in Safe Mode and this will be indicated in the top right hand corner.

When in Safe Mode, you can:

- Locate files you may want to store somewhere.

- Perform a system restore to return the computer to a more stable configuration.

If you use *Safe Mode with Networking*, you can access Internet resources, and use network connections to save files to a drive or folder on the network.

If you are using *Safe Mode with Command Prompt* you must log on with an administrator account.

Performing a system restore will be dealt with in more detail later on.

Server performance

> The performance monitor tracks a range of processes and applications, and provides a real time graphical display of them. In Windows this tool is known as *Perfmon*.

Using the performance monitor will help you to identify problems that may slow down your server. These can occur for a variety of reasons, including a hardware malfunction, software problem or an application trying to dominate a particular resource, for example, system memory.

Benefits of performance monitoring

Monitoring a network server's performance will help you better understand how server resources are being used and why performance is deteriorating. This will help you:

- Make the best use of resources, known as load balancing.

- Identify changes you can make to improve overall performance.

- Get alerted when resources are low.

- Identify the problems that are causing issues.

Choosing objects and counters

To monitor performance, you need to define:

- *Objects*: the items you monitor, for example, memory, processor or network interface.

- *Counters*: the aspect of performance that is monitored. The counters used will depend on the objects being monitored.

This section looks at how you can set up performance monitoring on your server.

Use the following steps to open the performance monitor and add a *Counter*:

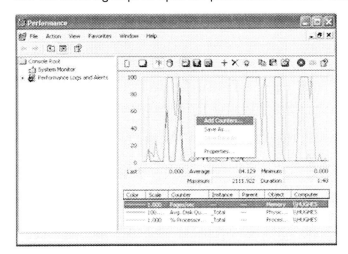

Actions

▶ 1. Click *Start*, select *Control Panel*, select *Administrative Tools* and select *Performance*.

▶ 2. A graph is displayed. Right-click on the graph and select *Add Counters*.

The *Add Counter* box offers the following options:

- *Computer*: this is the computer you are monitoring.

- *Object*: the subsystem being monitored, for example; memory, processor or the network interface.

- *Counter*: refers to the aspect of the object you want to monitor. This differs depending on the object.

- *Instance*: the specific object to be measured when multiple objects of the same type exist on a single system.

You should add counters for memory, processors, disks and networks. These are fundamental to the operation of any computer or server, so monitoring their activity will give you a good starting point to track down problems that might be occurring.

After that, you can add more counters to monitor specific aspects of the server's performance. Once you have added your counters, you can set the performance monitor's properties to allow you customise reports to view.

To adjust the properties, right-click on the graph and select *Properties*.

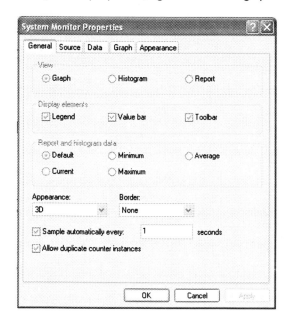

Actions

▶ 1. Right-click anywhere on the graph and choose *Properties*.

▶ 2. This brings up the *System Monitor Properties* window that will allow you to customise the appearance and settings when monitoring performance.

▶ 3. You can change the view to graph, report or histogram style, the monitoring time interval and the colour of the counter lines, amongst others.

The *System Monitor Properties* dialogue box provides the following tabs that allow you to:

- *General*: define the graph display, such as type of graph, elements that are displayed, and other general appearance options.

- *Source*: view current activity, activity stored in log files or view information stored in a database.

- *Data*: list the objects being monitored and define the colours representing them in the graph.

- *Graph*: provide a title for the graph, name the vertical axis, display grids and set minimum and maximum values for the grid.

- Appearance: define a colour for the graph background, and fonts used in the display.

Network related performance

Using the performance monitor can help you better understand the traffic flows and performance of your network. By monitoring objects such as the network interface, TCP (Transmission Control Protocol), and UDP (User Datagram Protocol), packet flow (these are protocols used to carry data around your network), you can identify how traffic moves around your network. To give just one example, by keeping a record of this activity, you can compare current information with historical data to identify at what point problems arose. This can help you identify whether adding a new piece of hardware or installing software has affected the network performance.

Performance logs and alerts

To monitor the performance of a simple server configuration, you need to collect three different types of performance data over a period of time:

General performance, basic performance and service level data can be collected to monitor performance.

- *General performance data*: is information that can help you identify short-term trends such as memory leaks. After a month or two of data collection, you can average the results and save them in a more compact format. This archived data can assist you in capacity planning.

- *Baseline performance data*: is information that can help you discover changes that occur slowly, over time. By comparing the current state of your system with historical data, you can troubleshoot and tune your system.

- *Data for service level reports*: is information that can help you ensure that your system meets a certain service or performance level, and which you will likely present to decision makers who are not performance analysts.

- *Alerts*: allow you to set an action that will be performed when specified counters reach a given value. For example you can use alerts to send out warnings when disk space is running low.

With the use of logs you are able to capture data that you can analyse later. Logged counter data information can be exported to spreadsheets and databases for future review and reporting.

You can use *Alerts* to send out warnings when disk space is running low or when network or level of CPU utilisation poses a risk.

Obtaining the IP address

> A ping is the process of sending a small amount of information to a specific IP address and asking the computer or device at that address to respond.

Ping tests are used to identify whether a computer or other device is connected to the network. You can use a ping test to identify connectivity problems with your network. Ping tests are also commonly used to measure the delay ('lag') with Internet servers.

To execute a ping test, you require the remote server / computer name or IP address.

The result of the ping test includes confirmation that a connection was successful, along with a series of numbers that represent the communication delay in milliseconds (ms).

The results of a ping test vary depending on the quality of the Internet / network connection.

You perform a ping test using a DOS prompt. Use the following steps to open the DOS interface:

> **Actions**
>
> ▶ 1. Click *Start*, select *Run*.
>
> ▶ 2. Type "cmd" in the *Open* field.
>
> ▶ 3. Click *OK*.

In the DOS prompt window type 'ping 'and the IP address of the device you wish to contact.

Four echo request packets are sent and the return times are shown if the test is successful. If you get the message 'Request timed out' your network interface card (NIC) is not responding to the echo requests. In the example below the test was successful.

```
E:\Windows\System32\command.com                          _ □ ×

E:\>ping 192.168.0.1

Pinging 192.168.0.1 with 32 bytes of data:

Reply from 192.168.0.1: bytes=32 time<1ms TTL=128
Reply from 192.168.0.1: bytes=32 time<1ms TTL=128
Reply from 192.168.0.1: bytes=32 time<1ms TTL=128
Reply from 192.168.0.1: bytes=32 time<1ms TTL=128

Ping statistics for 192.168.0.1:
    Packets: Sent = 4, Received = 4, Lost = 0 (0% loss),
Approximate round trip times in milli-seconds:
    Minimum = 0ms, Maximum = 0ms, Average = 0ms

E:\>
```

 A 'Request timed out' or a 'Destination host unreachable' message indicates that the ping test was not successful.

There are three common causes for a ping test to fail. These are:

- *Destination host unreachable*: means the computer or device you are trying to ping is not working, or is not connected to the network.

- *Request timed out*: means there was no reply from the host. This can happen because of heavy network traffic, route error or a connection problem.

- *Unknown host*: means the network does not recognise the IP address you are trying to ping.

Viewing in XP

Event viewer

> In Windows, an event is any significant occurrence in the system or in a program that requires users to be notified, or an entry added to a log.

The Event Log Service records application, security and system events in the Event Viewer.

Event logs can help you identify and diagnose the source of current system problems, or help you predict potential system problems.

Event log types

A Windows-based computer records events in the following three logs:

Application log

The application log contains events logged by programs. For example, a database program may record a file error in the application log.

Events that are written to the application log are determined by the developers of the software program.

Security log

The security log records events such as valid and invalid logon attempts, as well as events related to resource use, such as the creating, opening or deleting of files. For example, when log on auditing is enabled, an event is recorded in the security log each time a user attempts to log on to the computer.

You must be logged on as Administrator or as a member of the Administrators group in order to turn on, use, and specify which events are recorded in the security log.

System log

The system log contains events logged by Windows system components, for example, if a driver fails to load during startup, an event is recorded in the system log. Windows predetermines the events that are logged by system components.

Viewing event logs

Use the following steps to view event logs:

> ### Actions
>
> ▸ 1. Click *Start*, select *Control Panel*.
>
> ▸ 2. Click *Administrative Tools*.
>
> ▸ 3. Click *Computer Management* in the left pane.
>
> ▸ 4. Click on *System Tools* in the left pane.
>
> ▸ 5. Click on *Event Viewer* in the left pane.

How to view event details

A list of events is displayed in the right pane, click on any one to view the event.

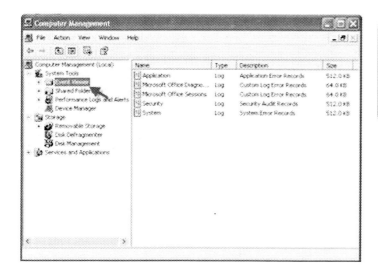

> ### Actions
>
> ▸ 1. Click on the *Event Viewer* and click on the relevant log to access the information.

How to interpret an event

Each log entry is classified by type, and contains header information and a description of the event.

The event header contains the following information about the event:

- *Date*: the date the event occurred.

- *Time*: the time the event occurred.

- *User*: the user name of the user that was logged on when the event occurred.

- *Computer*: the name of the computer where the event occurred.

- *Event ID*: an event number that identifies the event type. The Event ID can be used by product support representatives to help understand what occurred in the system.

- *Source*: the source of the event. This can be the name of a program, a system component, or an individual component of a large program.

- *Type*: the type of event. This can be one of the following five types: Error, Warning, Information, Success Audit or Failure Audit.

- *Category*: a classification of the event by the event source. This is primarily used in the security log.

- *Event Types*: the description of each event that is logged depends on the type of event. Each event in a log can be classified into one of the following types:

- *Information*: an event that describes the successful operation of a task, such as an application driver or service. For example, an *Information* event is logged when a network driver loads successfully.

- *Warning*: an event indicating a potential future problem

- *An error*: an event that is a significant problem, for example data loss.

Viewing logs in Vista

In Vista you can open the Event Viewer by:

Actions

▶ 1. Right-clicking on the *Computer* icon on the desktop.

▶ 2. Click *Manage*.

▶ 3. Click *System Tools*.

▶ 4. Click *Event Viewer*.

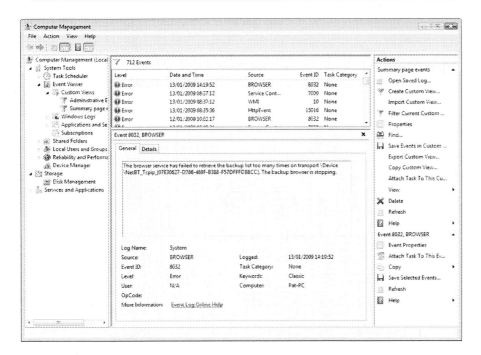

 Note that, with a glance, you can easily view the number of errors, warnings etc, under different views such as for the past 24 hours or 7 days.

Backup and restore

> A data backup is a copy of all the files on a computer or other storage devices. The backup is stored on another computer, server or storage device so that the information can be retrieved should the original device fail.

To give an example, there are tools that can run in the background to create backups of files. This would maintain a full data backup and allow for retrieval at a later date.

> A system backup restores the computer to a previously defined state, as well all the local settings and configurations.

System imaging tools create a backup of an entire computer drive, so that you can quickly restore an operating system and all the applications in the event of a computer crash or total system failure.

Backups are used to restore information that has been lost due to physical damage to storage media, malicious or accidental corruption of data, or the failure of the computer system.

This failure can be caused by:

- Natural disasters, for example fires or floods.

- Human intervention, for example someone deleting information.

- Computer viruses corrupting or deleting information or making it inaccessible.

- Computer(s) breaking down.

Most organisations could not continue to operate if they lost important internal or customer information.

When making backups, there are a number of good practice guidelines you should follow.

Make backups of your files regularly, so that if you need to restore information, the backup is as close as possible to an exact copy of the information that has been lost.

Create multiple backups, in case one becomes compromised or fails.

Keep at least one backup offsite. If a backup is stored in the same location as the original information and a fire breaks out, both can be destroyed and all your information will be lost.

To make the backup process easier, you should ensure everyone saves their files to a shared drive on a dedicated computer or network server. This way, you can be sure you are backing up the entire organisation's important information when you perform a backup on a shared drive or folder.

Backup XP

Windows provides a *Backup or Restore Wizard* to help make backups and restore lost information quickly and easily.

In order to start a backup:

> ## Actions
>
> ▸ 1. Click *Start*, select *All Programs*.
>
> ▸ 2. Click *Accessories*, select *System Tools*
>
> ▸ 3. Click *Backup*. The *Restore Wizard* is displayed, click *Next*.
>
> ▸ 4. Select the *Backup and settings* option and click *Next*.
>
> ▸ 5. Click *Backup files and settings*.

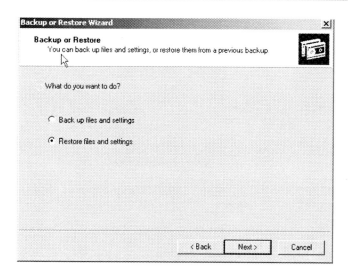

In the *What to Back Up* area select from one of the following options:

- *My documents and settings*: saves this information only, including favourites, desktop settings and cookies.

- *Everyone's documents and settings*: saves information for all profiles on the computer. Select this option if there are multiple users and you want to backup the information on this computer.

- *All information on this computer*: saves everything on the computer's hard drive. It is recommended not to do this, as the resulting file will be needlessly large, as it will contain information that you may never need.

- *Let me choose what to back up*: allows you to identify specific folders or locations to create a backup from. Enable this option when backing up a shared folder or network drive.

Be cautious with the *All information on this computer* option, particularly if the computer has a lot of software already installed.

For most users, the *My documents and settings* option is a better choice. This selection preserves your data files (including email messages and address books) and the personal settings stored in the Windows Registry.

If several users use a computer, select *Everyone's documents and settings*. This option backs up personal files and preferences for every user with an account on the computer.

If some of your files are on a shared network drive, open the *My Network Places* folder and select those folders.

Once you have identified what you want to backup, you will need to specify where to save the backup to.

Windows will create your backup as a single file that can be saved to a specific location. This could be:

- A CD/DVD in the CD drive.

- The hard drive.

- A removable storage device, like a USB key.

- A network drive or folder.

- An external hard drive.

Click the *Browse* button to specify the location where you want to store your backup. If you select the hard drive or a network drive or folder, you should remember to take a copy of it to keep off site.

Also provide a name for your backup. It is good practice to include the date and a brief (one word if possible) description of what is backed up. To give an example, *2009_Accounts*.

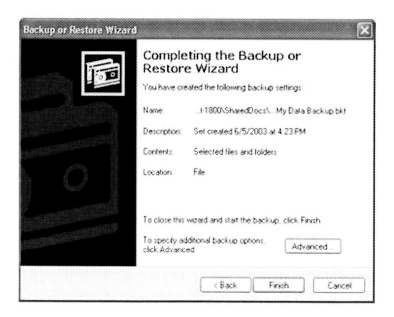

Advanced backup options

There are additional backup options available by clicking the *Advanced* button above the finish button in the *Backup and Restore Wizard*.

The backup options include backup validation, backup compression and the options to add to or overwrite existing backups. Also you can set a backup schedule.

Set a schedule

It is good practice to take regular backups of shared drives and folders on the network. How often you need to take backups will depend on how much information is generated by your organisation and how often. However, you should take a backup at least once a week and ensure there is a backup policy within your organisation.

To set a schedule:

> Actions
>
> ▸ 1. In the *Backup and Restore Wizard*, click *Advanced* on the final page instead of *Finish*.
>
> ▸ 2. Click *Next* and make your required choices, until you reach the *When to Back Up* page.
>
> ▸ 3. Click *Later* and enter a job name and select *Set Schedule*. Enter the required time and date and complete the process.

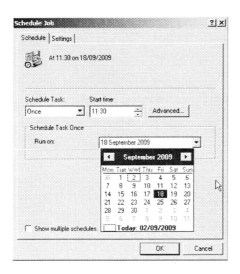

You can specify a range of details, including:

- The frequency of backups (daily, weekly, monthly, whenever the computer is idle, at startup, etc).

- A specified time, where the frequency is daily, weekly or monthly.

- Specific days for a weekly backup.

- A specific day in a month for a monthly backup, and even specific months.

It is good practice to keep your backup schedule simple: back up either daily or weekly, with a time that people are less likely to be using the computer or network resource that you are backing up.

Finally, click *OK* to save your changes.

 There is a wide range of backup utilities available on the market. Many are developed to backup specific types of information, for example, email, or to backup from specific types of media, for example network drives. If you want to create backups like these, it is worth investigating the tools available, as they are often more efficient than the utilities built into computers.

Alternative backups

While it is good practice to schedule regular backups of your organisation's information, it is important to note that this is not the only kind of backup you can create.

There is a range of tools you can use to create more specific backups. To give an example, there are tools that can run in the background to create backups of emails. This is a useful tool where working files and documents are stored to a shared drive or folder. Creating a backup of the email communications would be light on the computer's resources, but also ensure you have a copy of all the organisation's email communications.

There are also drive imaging tools, which can be useful where you want to create a backup of an entire computer's drive. This is good to have if you need to be able to quickly restore an operating system and all the applications on a computer in case it crashes.

Restoring a backup, XP

Use the following to restore a backup:

Actions

▶ 1. In the *Backup and Restore Wizard,* select the *Restore and settings* option and click *Next.*

▶ 2. In *What to Restore,* click on the + symbol by the file(s) you wish to restore and select the relevant check boxes or click *Browse* to locate the required files. Click *Next.*

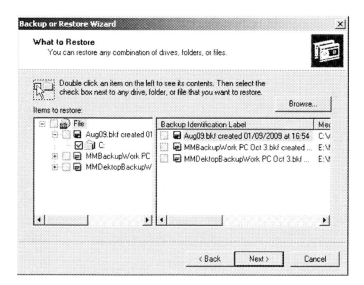

In the *Advanced* options:

Actions

▶ 1. In the *Where to Restore* page, you can select a location for the restore file(s). Click *Next.*

- Select *Original location* to restore files to their original folder/drives.

- Select *Alternate location* if the files have been moved.

- Select *Single Folder* to restore all files to a single folder.

▶ 2. In the *How to Restore* page, choose how you want to restore files where they already exist and click *Next.*

- *Enable Leave existing files* to prevent existing files from being overwritten.

- *Enable Replace existing files* to overwrite the files on the computer.

▶ 3. Accept the default *Advanced Restore Options,* click *Next* and click *Finish* to start the restore.

This process will restore information you have backed up from a network or other drive. You would use this where information has been deleted, or a computer has been destroyed or stolen and you need to access the information that was stored on it.

Windows XP system restore

A System Restore is different to a backup restore. A backup restore will replace files that have been specifically backed up. A System Restore will return the computer to a previous configuration.

System Restore is used where a computer has started acting strangely, become unstable or unresponsive. The usual cause for this is a conflict in software or hardware that has recently been added to the computer.

Using System Restore will allow you to return the computer to a configuration that you know was working prior to installing the software or hardware.

The System Restore utility automatically creates restore points on your computer. These are system backups, which are snapshots of your computer's configuration, including hardware setup, applications and application settings as well as other settings. You can restore the computer's configuration to one of these restore points. This means the computer will 'forget' any applications or hardware installed between creating the restore point and the time you restore. Files stored on your computer are not affected by this.

System Restore requires at least 200MB of disc space. If this is not available, the utility will not work. Over time, you may need to allocate more space to System Restore to allow it to save the different applications, settings and hardware profiles on your computer. Use the following steps to do this:

Actions

▶ 1. Click *Start*, select *Control Panel*.

▶ 2. Select *System*.

▶ 3. Click *System Restore*.

▶ 4. Click the *Drive* where the System Restore will be saved.

▶ 5. Drag the slider to the right to increase the amount of space System Restore can use.

 A range of system backup and restore tools are also widely available. These allow you to take an image of your drive, which will not only backup files, but also the operating system and any applications and configuration settings. You can then restore the entire system from the last drive image you took.

System Restore should only be used after trying less comprehensive methods of troubleshooting. System Restore changes many files and registry entries, and in some cases might replace more files than you want restored.

Using system restore

If your computer has become unstable or unresponsive and you want to perform a system restore, you may need to boot it into safe mode.

Use the following steps to restore your computer to a previous configuration.

Actions

▶ 1. Click *Start* , select *All Programs*, select *Accessories*.

▶ 2. Click *System Tools*, select *System Restore*.

▶ 3. Enable the *Restore my computer to an earlier time* option under *What do you want to do?*

▶ 4. Select a Restore point from the dates displayed on the calendar.

▶ 5. Click *Next*.

▶ 6. Click *Next* to confirm the restore point you have selected.

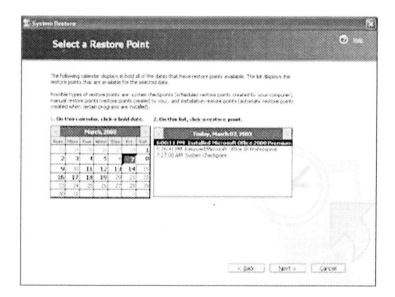

The computer will restart, with its configuration restored to the point you have chosen. When the computer has booted up, a message will confirm that the system restore was successful. Click *OK* to continue.

You can then monitor the computer's stability, and either:

• Keep the restore point configuration.

• Try another restore point configuration.

• Undo the restore.

These instructions cover system restore using Windows XP System Restore utility.

Advanced backup and restore

Windows Vista Business, Ultimate, and Enterprise come with a more advanced backup and restore utility called Windows Complete PC Backup and Restore.

Windows Vista offers an integrated system and file backup system. This is known as Windows Complete PC Backup and Restore. This utility creates an image of the hard disk, which allows you to restore specific files, or the complete system in case of a major failure.

Use the following steps to access the *Backup and Restore Centre*:

1. Click *Start*, select *All Programs*.

2. Click *Maintenance*, select *Backup and Restore Centre*.

From here you can create backups, schedule regular backups and restore files or the entire system.

Unlike the standard back up and restore feature that comes with all the versions of Windows Vista, Windows Complete PC Backup and Restore allows you not only to restore the data but also the complete operating system and other critical system files.

To create a backup:

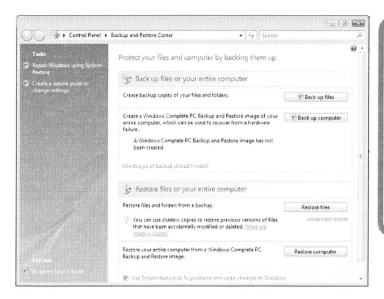

Actions

▶ 1. Click on the *Start* button, click *All Programs*.

▶ 2. Click on the *Maintenance* folder.

▶ 3. Click on the *Backup and Restore Center* icon.

▶ 4. The *Windows Complete PC Backup* Wizard will now appear.

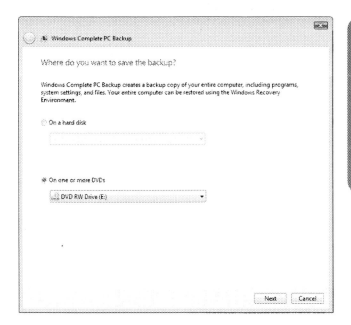

Actions

▶ 5. Click *Backup computer*.

▶ 6. You should choose where you want to save the backup, on a hard disk or set of DVDs, click *Next*.

▶ 7. Confirm your additional backup settings and click *Start backup*.

It is vital that you check your backups have been taken correctly when they are saved. Some commercial backup utilities will include a feature that does this automatically.

It is also good practice to restore backups to another computer that did not store the original information, and access files randomly. This will let you know whether the information has been copied successfully.

Rotational backup schemes

A rotational backup stores backups to different physical media on a regular basis.

An example of rotational backups is to take a backup of information and store it to a server. The next day, a backup is taken again. This time, the backup is stored to a hard drive, which is removed to another location once the backup has been stored. On the third day, a backup is taken and stored using an online service. On the fourth day, the backup is stored on the server again, replacing the first backup. You can schedule several backups to do this using the steps outlined above.

Using rotational backups adds a level of security to your backup process. Taking regular backups means the information stored is always current. Storing the backups to different physical media means that if any one media fails, a recent backup can be restored from another media.

The complexity of your rotational backup system will depend on the amount of information stored on your network and its sensitivity. Some organisations will store backups to multiple media at the same time, ensuring the most current backup is available from a range of sources.

Off site backups

> Offsite, or remote, backups are stored in a different location to the computers or equipment that hold the information.

Offsite backups can be taken by saving data to a drive that is physically removed from the organisation's premises.

Alternatively, there are many online services, which will allow you to backup information over the Internet. If you plan to use such a service, you should have a good broadband connection, so that the backup can be taken quickly and efficiently. You should also check the backup company's recovery procedures to ensure your information is kept safe in the event of a power blackout, fire, flood, or other disaster.

Power supply issues

Introduction

Power supply issues can cause serious problems for computer and network equipment. Not only are components powered by electricity, data is transmitted and processed as electrical signals.

Two common power issues you need to address are:

- Electrical surges, where excess power is allowed into a computer or other device.
- Power cuts.

This section looks at surge protectors and Uninterruptible Power Supply (UPS) systems, which can be used to defend your equipment from these issues. You can increasingly buy surge protectors and UPS systems in one unit.

Surge protector

> A surge protector is a piece of equipment used to protect electrical products from voltage spikes.

A surge protector is designed to regulate the electricity being delivered to electrical equipment. An electrical surge can affect computers or devices in two ways:

- By wearing or even destroying electrical components.
- By corrupting or making data in transit or stored on drives unreadable.

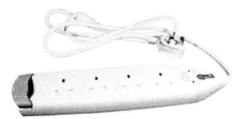

Surges have a variety of causes, from local electrical equipment starting up, and faulty wiring to random spikes in the electrical supply line.

A surge protector will divert excess power to a grounding wire, which prevents it affecting electrical equipment.

It is good practice to ensure all computer and network equipment is plugged into a surge protector to prevent damage to equipment or loss of data. You should also buy surge protectors that include a light to let you know the surge protector is working.

Surge protectors cannot defend against surges caused by lightning. To protect against a lightening storm, you should backup all files and unplug as much as possible any computers or network equipment that store vital information. If some equipment cannot be unplugged, ensure you have a full backup of the information stored on it.

Uninterruptible Power Supply (UPS)

An Uninterruptible Power Supply (UPS) stores electricity in a battery to provide continuous power in the case of a blackout.

If the power is cut to a computer, all the information stored in RAM and being transmitted will be lost. Using a UPS will provide a period of time for people to store the information in RAM and shut down their computer normally. Many advanced UPS systems now provide software that will automate a backup and safe shutdown in case of a power cut when you are not there.

There are two types of UPS system:

- Standby power systems (SPS).

- Online UPS.

Standby power systems will switch to battery power once a power outage is detected. This can take as little as a few milliseconds. However, in this time, a computer may have lost power and shut down unexpectedly.

Online UPS prevents this by continuously providing power from its own battery. If the main electricity source is cut, power from the battery keeps the computer operating normally and provides time to save information and shut down properly.

Quick Quiz

Select the correct answer from the following multiple-choice questions:

1   What is a 'clean' installation?

   a   Reinstalling software on a brand new computer

   b   Installing software onto a computer for the first time

   c   Reinstalling software onto a computer once its hard disk has been repartitioned and reformatted

   d   An installation of software over an already installed version

2   What kind of file has the file suffix .ini?

   a   Temporary

   b   Application

   c   System

   d   Data

3   Under which circumstances are multiple partitions needed on a hard disk?

   a   To ensure data security

   b   To run Windows

   c   To run Windows in safe mode

   d   To run multiple operating systems

4   What is loaded on Windows in Safe Mode?

   a   The minimum processes needed to start Windows

   b   All processes except those recently installed

   c   All processes except those which access the Internet

   d   The default settings installed onto the computer when it was sold

5   Complete the following sentence by inserting the missing word from the options below.

   You can use a _____ test to troubleshoot connectivity problems in a network.

   a   Ping

   b   Zip

   c   Views

   d   Data

Answers to Quick Quiz

1   c   Reinstalling software onto a computer once its hard disk has been repartitioned and reformatted

2   c   System

3   d   To run multiple operating systems

4   a   The minimum processes required to start Windows

5   a   Ping

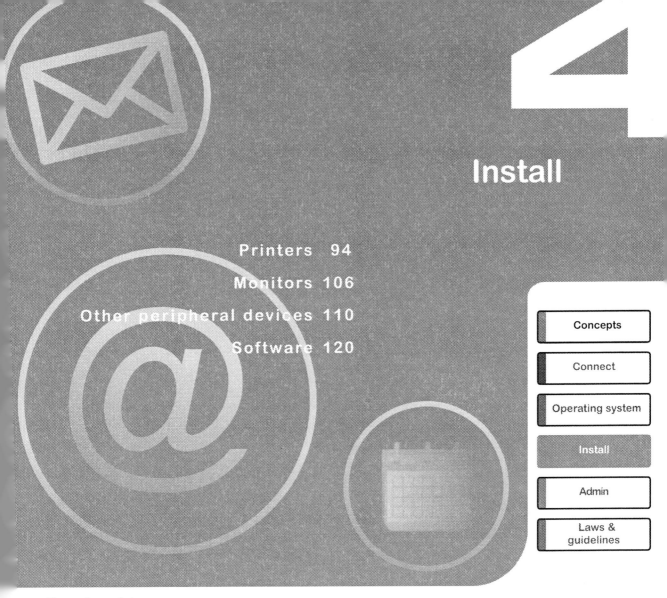

Concepts

Connect

Operating system

Install

Admin

Laws &
guidelines

Measuring points

▶ Identify different printer types: dot matrix, laser, ink jet
▶ Be able to install different printers
▶ Know how to add, modify, remove a printer
▶ Control permissions for a shared printer
▶ Cancel, pause, re-start a print job
▶ Be able to troubleshoot everyday printer problems
▶ Be able to replace printer consumables and clean printers
▶ Recognise different monitor types. Identify factors which can impact display quality such as resolution, refresh rate, number of colours used
▶ Be able to install different monitors
▶ Know how to change settings such as resolution, refresh rate, number of colours displaying
▶ Connect an overhead protector to a local machine

▶ Install a modem or other communications device
▶ Install different peripheral devices such as scanners, CD-ROM drive, additional memory, memory expansion cards, sound cards, network interface cards
▶ Be able to install different Plug 'n' Play devices
▶ Be able to add different assistive technology devices
▶ Recognise that all components consume power
▶ Recognise that cleaning peripherals helps maintain efficiency
▶ Be able to install Internet browser, email software
▶ Be able to install applications software
▶ Be able to install different utility software (backup, diagnostic, anti virus)
▶ Be able to remove different kinds of applications software
▶ Install, remove or maintain different device, network driver sets

Introduction

This chapter covers the installation and troubleshooting tasks you may be involved with when connecting and maintaining printers and monitors.

Printers and monitors are some of the most widely used computer peripherals and are an important part of network administration.

Printers

This section deals with printers and how you can install them for use with a specific computer or on a network. This chapter looks at these three common printer types:

- Dot matrix

- Laser

- Ink jet

Dot matrix

A dot matrix printer works by striking pins against an ink ribbon to print characters on a page.

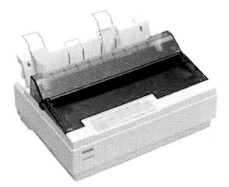

The main characteristics of dot matrix printers are:

- Creates letters and shapes on paper by building up a series of dots.

- Popular for home use and small offices.

- Fast and efficient but noisy.

- Older technology superseded by laser and inkjet printers.

Laser printer

A laser printer creates a static charge on a drum, which is then coated in toner, which is a dry ink. Paper is then fed through the machine to create an imprint on it.

The main characteristics of laser printers are:

- Popular because prices are becoming more competitive but still top of the range.

- Print image dries immediately and, no smearing of print.

- Larger models are used in offices to print large volumes of documents.

Inkjet printer

An inkjet printer sprays ink from a series of different coloured cartridge heads onto paper at high speed.

The main characteristics of Inkjet printers are:

- Popular because they are quite cheap. Often delivered as part of home computer package.

- Light and easy to transport.

- High quality printing, up to 300dpi.

- Use ink cartridges, which are an expense. Manufacturers make their profits from the sale of ink cartridges.

- Prone to smearing, as ink needs to dry.

Installing printers

When installing a new printer with the *Add Printer Wizard*, you can choose between adding a local printer or a network printer.

This section outlines the process for installing a local printer using the *Add New Printer Wizard*.

To connect effectively to a printer, a computer needs a physical or wireless connection to the printer and some software to manage the connection and interpret the various commands exchanged with the printer. This software is termed a printer driver. Different printers from a range of suppliers all need different drivers, their particular driver, to operate. The right driver has to be installed in the computer for the printer to work.

The drivers for most printers are already installed on Microsoft XP and Vista operating systems. However, it is good practice before purchasing a printer to confirm that it is compatible with the computer you will be using it with.

If the drivers are not already installed on your OS, you can use an installation CD. However, if you buy a Plug and Play compatible printer, Windows will install it for you.

Whichever option you choose, to install a printer, you need to access the *Add New Printer* Wizard:

Actions

▶ 1. Click *Start*, select *Control Panel*.

- In XP, click on *Printers and Faxes*.

- In Vista, click *Printers* under *Hardware and Sounds*.

▶ 2. Select *Add a Printer*.

- In XP, this is in the left pane.

- In Vista, this is on the toolbar at the top of the window.

▶ 3. Click *Next* in the *Add New Printer Wizard*.

▶ 4. Select the type of printer, for example if a local printer: enable the *Local printer attached to this computer option* and click the *Automatically detect and install my Pug and Play Device* option.

▶ 5. If your printer is a recognised Plug and Play device and connected to your computer, Windows will install it automatically.

If Windows cannot install the printer itself, it will display a page asking you to install it manually. To do this, you will need to know the port that the printer is plugged into, the printer model and also provide a name for it. Click *Next* to do install the printer manually:

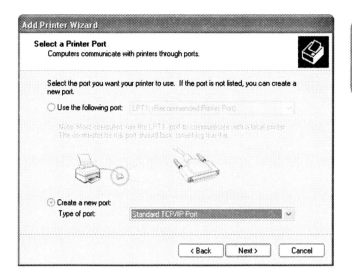

Actions

▸ 2. In the *Install Printer Software* area, click the printer manufacturer in the left pane and click the printer model in the right pane. If the manufacturer or model is not listed, you can either:

- Click *Windows Update* to see if a driver is available online.

- Click *Have Disk* to install the printer driver from a CD or USB key.

▸ 3. Click *Next* to install the print drivers.

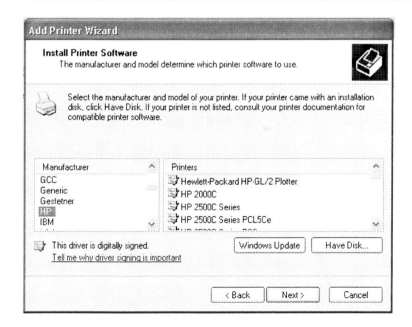

▶ 4. If you have a disk with the software for the printer, put it into the CD-ROM drive and then click the *Have Disk* button.

▶ 5. Select the drive that contains this disk in the *Copy Manufacturer's Files* drop-down list box and then click *OK*.

▶ 6. Click the *Next* button to advance to the *Name Your Printer* dialogue box.

▶ 7. If you want, edit the name for the printer in the *Printer Name* text box, print a test page, click *Finish*.

If you want to make the printer that you are installing the default printer that is automatically used whenever you print from Windows or from within a Windows program, leave the *Yes* radio button selected beneath the heading.

If you want to share this printer with other users on the network, click the *Share Name* button and then, if you want, edit the share name (this is the name that the other users on the network see when they go to select this printer for printing their documents) that the wizard gives the printer in the *Share Name* text box.

Removing a printer

When you remove a printer from your network, it is good practice to remove it from your computer as well. Use the following steps to do this:

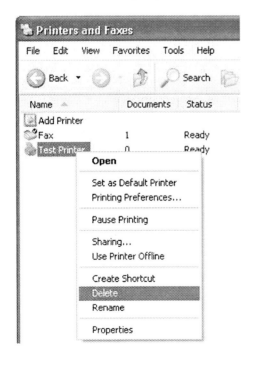

Actions

▶ 1. Click *Start*, select *Printers and Faxes*.

▶ 2. Right-click on the printer you want to remove.

▶ 3. Click *Delete*.

▶ 4. Click *Yes* in the *Confirmation* dialogue box.

When you are removing a printer, you may also need to remove extra drivers or support software that was installed with it. Use the following steps to do this:

Actions

▶ 1. Click *Start*, select *Control Panel*.

▶ 2. Click *Add or Remove Programs*.

▶ 3. Click on the application you want to remove.

▶ 4. Click *Change / Remove*.

To modify a printer so it is the default printer, right-click it and select *Set as Default*.

Printer sharing

When sharing a printer, you can define whether extra drivers will be needed (for example, if people using different operating systems will be using the printer), and define user permissions for the printer.

Defining permissions involves specifying the level of control users have over the printer. For example, they may only be allowed to print (basic level), or they may be allowed to manage the printer and define permissions for other users (administrative level).

Defining whether extra drivers are required, as well as permissions, are addressed in the instructions provided below.

You can share a printer with anyone else in the network by using the following steps:

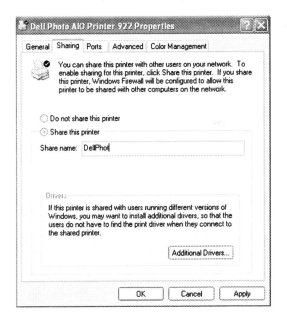

Actions

▶ 1. Click *Start*, select *Control Panel*.

▶ 2. Click *Printers and Faxes*.

▶ 3. Right-click on the printer you want to share.

▶ 4. Click *Sharing*.

If users sharing the printer use different hardware or have a different operating system, you need to install extra drivers so they will be able to use the printer. Use the following steps to do this:

To stop sharing your printer

Use the following steps to stop sharing a printer:

Setting or removing permissions

Permissions allow you to define who can use a printer and the level of control they have over it. Organisations often apply permissions to only allow certain people to use a printer. An example of this is sharing a printer among a specific group of people. This makes it easier to manage network and printer resources.

Use the following steps to set permissions for a printer:

Actions

▶ 1. Click *Start*, select *Control Panel*, select *Printers and Faxes*.

▶ 2. Right-click on the printer you want to apply permissions for.

▶ 3. Select *Properties*.

▶ 4. Click the *Security* tab.

Actions

▶ 5. Click *Add*.

▶ 6. Click *Look For*, select the types of users you want to add, and then click *OK*.

▶ 7. Click *Look In*, browse for the location you want to search, and then click *OK*.

▶ 8. In the *Name* box, type the name of the user or group you want to set permissions for, separating each name with a semicolon (;).

▶ 9. To ensure the names are recognised by the directory, click *Check Names*.

▶ 10. Once all the names you require are listed in the *Name* box, click *OK*.

▶ 11. In *Permissions*, click the *Allow or Deny* check box for each permission you want to allow or deny.

▶ 12. To view or change the underlying printer permissions that make up *Print, Manage Printers*, and *Manage Documents*, click *Advanced*.

There are four types of printer permissions:

- *Print*: allows a specified group or person to print.

- *Manage documents*: allows the user to manage the document queue to the printer (for example, cancelling printing for a document, or giving it priority over other documents.

- *Manage printers*: allows the user to set preferences for the printer, such as naming it, sharing it or even deleting it.

- *Special permissions*: are advanced administrative permissions. These are usually only given to the administrator or owner of the printer.

You can define exactly what each of these permissions mean by clicking the *Advanced* button.

Once the group or users you want to add permissions for are listed, click *OK*. The group or users you added will be displayed in the top pane of the *Security* tab.

To change or remove permissions, click on the group or user name in the top pane of the *Security* tab, and disable the appropriate options in the bottom pane.

In Windows Vista, you can define printer permissions from the *Properties* dialogue box for the printer. To access this, right-click on the printer, and select *Properties*. The permissions can be defined under the *Sharing* tab.

Managing the print queue

Controlling print jobs is a useful way to manage printer resources. When documents are sent to a printer, they are added to a print queue. This establishes an order in which the documents will be printed. Generally, the print queue will work on a first come, first served basis. However, you can intervene to pause, cancel or restart a print.

Access the *Printers and Faxes* dialogue box from the *Control Panel* in XP and double-click on the printer you want to manage. Right-click on a document and select the action you want to perform:

- *Pause*: will stop the document from being printed, giving priority to another document in the queue.

- *Restart*: will restart the print on a paused document.

- *Cancel*: will delete the document from the print queue altogether.

- *Properties*: will allow you to adjust the printer's set up, as outlined above.

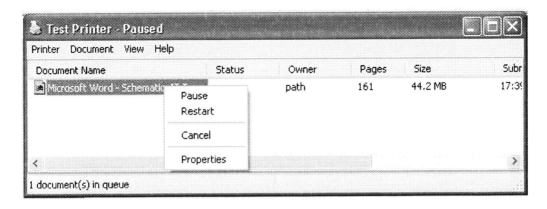

Troubleshooting printer problems

The Windows Printing Troubleshooter tool can help you resolve common printer problems. This is a help file that allows you to find out about common printer installation and operational problems.

If you have problems with your printer, the *Help and Support Center* is a valuable resource you can use to identify and rectify it.

Use the following steps to access the *Printer Troubleshooting* section of the *Help and Support Center*:

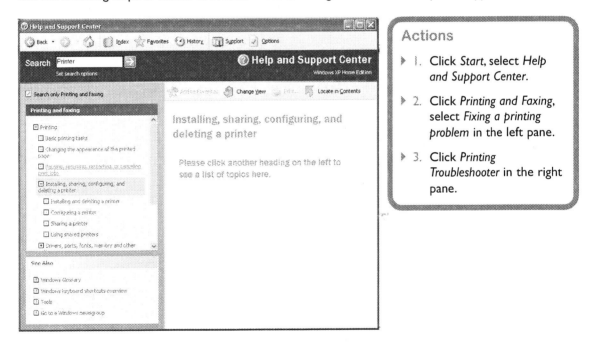

Actions

▶ 1. Click *Start*, select *Help and Support Center*.

▶ 2. Click *Printing and Faxing*, select *Fixing a printing problem* in the left pane.

▶ 3. Click *Printing Troubleshooter* in the right pane.

The *Help and Support Center* provides useful information on a variety of problems, not just printing. You can use it as a resource to identify actions you can take for a range of problems you may encounter with the computer.

Replacing printer ink

The following are general guidelines and will vary from printer to printer.

Most printers will let you know they are running out of ink in two ways:

- If there is a display on the printer, a warning will be displayed.

- When printing, a message will be displayed on your computer.

When you receive a low ink warning, you can continue to use the printer, but it is good practice to ensure you have spare ink cartridges ready.

The mechanisms used to access printer cartridges vary from printer to printer. Consult your printer manual for specific instructions for the printer.

You can generally remove an ink cartridge by gently pushing it down in the printer carriage. It will pop back up and out of the print carriage. You can then lift the cartridge out. Before removing and inserting an ink cartridge, you should refer to the printer's manual to ensure this is the proper process. Some printers include locks and other mechanisms to hold cartridges in place. These need to be disabled before trying to remove the cartridge.

To insert a new cartridge, remove it from its packaging, being careful not to touch any connectors or exposed parts. Most cartridges have a black plastic band around them, which you should use to hold and carry the cartridge. Gently push the new cartridge into place.

If you are changing multiple cartridges, it is good practice to change them one at a time, rather than taking out all the cartridges, then inserting all the new ones. This will prevent you placing a cartridge into the wrong slot, which would cause the colours to print incorrectly.

Caution: Do not touch the copper-coloured contacts or ink nozzles. Touching these parts can result in clogs, ink failure, and bad electrical connections.

Printer maintenance

Every printer needs an occasional tune-up, particularly if it has not been used for a long time. The maintenance process consumes ink, so don't use it unless necessary.

When printouts become faint or certain colours fail to print, use the nozzle check utility to test whether the print heads are working properly. If the printout shows gaps, clean the nozzles.

This process removes blockages in the nozzles. Sometimes cleaning needs to be performed more than once.

Nozzle check

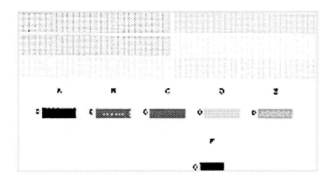

In some printers you can perform a nozzle check. Select *Properties*, click *Maintenance* and click *Nozzle test*.

The printer will print a page consisting of blocks of colours. You should check this for unevenness or missing lines, as these could be signs that your print heads need aligning.

Print head alignment

Your print heads may require alignment if:

- There are strange marks printed on pages.

- Text is unevenly placed on a page.

- Colours are blurred, or you can see the primary colours used to create a colour (for example, you see red and yellow instead of orange).

Many printers require you to use a special card or type of paper to perform the head alignment. You should refer to your printer's manual for more information.

In some printer's, you can perform a print head alignment from the maintenance page in the *Printer Properties* dialogue box. Select *Maintenance* tab, then click *Printer head alignment*.

General maintenance

There are a number of routine tasks you should perform to maintain a printer. This will help to extend its life and ensure it works well.

Manually clean the printer. Make sure the printer is unplugged. Open the printer and use a dry lint-free cloth to gently wipe away any accumulated dust or stray drops of ink.

Update drivers. If your printer is a bit older than your computer you may need to check for driver updates or patches. Visit the manufacturer's website and look on the tech support page for any relevant downloads.

If you have a paper jam always refer to the manual for the safest method of clearing jams.

If cleaning and alignment do not solve a problem, contact the manufacturer for the cost of repair. If your printer is no longer covered under warranty, assess whether repair costs are worth it.

When buying a new printer, you will need to consider that while the cost of the printer itself could be low, additional costs will be incurred through frequent cartridge replacement. The number of pages each cartridge produces should be an important aspect of the purchasing decision.

Monitors

This section outlines how to install, adjust the settings for and uninstall a monitor.

There is a range of monitors available on the market. The most common are CRT (Cathode Ray Tube) and TFT-LCD (Thin Film Transistor Liquid Crystal Display). CRT monitors are larger, and work in a similar way to televisions. TFT-LCD monitors have become more popular as they have a smaller size and a clearer display.

In most cases, simply plugging the display into the correct outlet is enough to get you up and running.

However, a range of options can be used to get the optimum performance from your monitor. These settings can make working with the monitor easier on the eye for users. The settings that can be adjusted are discussed later in this section and include the screen resolution, refresh rate and area size.

However, installing a monitor so that you get the optimum performance and flexibility from it, is another matter. Even advanced users often neglect the finer points of optimising a display.

Uninstall a monitor

When you are removing a monitor, it is good practice to uninstall its drivers from the computer. This avoids conflicts arising between drivers or software. You should uninstall the old monitor after you have installed the new one.

Use the following steps to uninstall a monitor:

> Actions
>
> ▸ 1. Click *Start*, select *Control Pane*.
>
> ▸ 2. Click *System*.
>
> ▸ 3. Click *Hardware*.
>
> ▸ 4. Click the *Device Manager* button.
>
> ▸ 5. In the *Device Manager*, select *Monitors*.
>
> ▸ 6. Right-click the model of your monitor and click *Uninstall*.

Some monitors provide a utility application that lets you control them. It is good practice to remove this application when uninstalling a monitor. Use the following steps to do this:

Install a new monitor

Before connecting a new monitor to a computer, you should install any drivers that came with the monitor.

If the monitor is Plug and Play compatible, you should be able to just plug it in and start the computer.

You should check the monitor's manual to identify any specific actions or steps you need to take when installing it.

Before connecting your new monitor, make sure the computer is not plugged into an electrical outlet.

Find the correct connector to connect the monitor to the computer. This is usually situated on the back panel of the computer.

Once the monitor has been plugged into the appropriate connector, tighten the thumbscrews on the connector to ensure the connection is secure.

If you are using a DVI (Digital Video Interface) adaptor, make sure that both the adaptor and the VGA (Video Graphics Array) connectors from the monitor are screwed securely together and into the video card. This ensures that all pins in the adaptor make proper contact.

Plug the monitor's power cord into a surge protector. Monitors are sensitive to damage from power spikes and surges, so investing in a good surge protector is important.

Once you have connected the monitor to the computer, plug in the monitor and computer (and any other connected devices that require electrical power) and switch on the computer.

Turn on the monitor's power switch. One of two things will happen.

• The computer will start normally, in which case the monitor has been successfully installed.

• The computer will start and Windows will display a *Found New Hardware Wizard.*

If the *Found New Hardware Wizard* starts, click *Next*, and follow the instructions to install the monitor. This may include inserting a CD with the monitor's drivers, or locating the drivers on the computer.

Display settings

There are a range of options you can use to optimise the monitor's display and performance. One typical setting you should adjust is the display resolution. Once the monitor is installed, Windows will normally use a resolution defined in the drivers.

To adjust the display resolution:

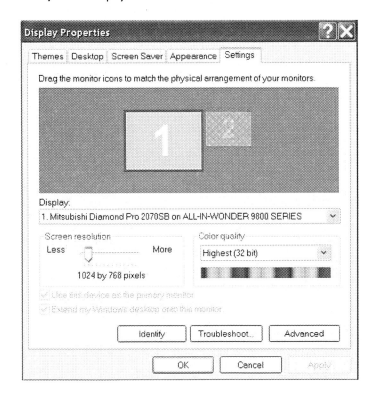

Actions

▶ 1. Right-click on the desktop and click *Properties*.

▶ 2. Click the *Settings* tab.

▶ 3. Drag the slide to the left to lower, or right to increase the display resolution.

▶ 4. Click *Apply*.

The resolution will change; making items on the screen appear larger or smaller. Windows will ask if you want to keep the changes.

Click *Yes* to keep the changes, or *No* to revert to the original resolution.

Refreshing

For CRT monitors, the refresh rate setting is the number of times the display card redraws the image on the screen every second.

A low refresh rate creates flicker on a display, which leads to eyestrain.

Each display resolution has a corresponding range of refresh rates at which the resolution can operate safely. You should check with the manual for the optimum resolution and refresh rate for your monitor.

Use the following steps to adjust the monitor's refresh rate.

Actions

▶ 1. Open the *Display Properties* dialogue box as outlined previously.

▶ 2. Click the *Settings* tab.

▶ 3. Click the *Advanced* button.

▶ 4. Click the *Monitor* tab.

▶ 5. In the *Monitor settings* section, enable the *Hide modes that this monitor cannot* display option.

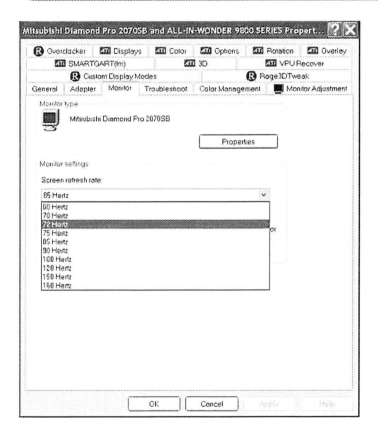

Actions

▶ 6. Now use the *Screen Refresh Rate* drop-down menu to highlight the appropriate rate and click *Apply*.

 Setting a refresh rate of 72Hz or 75Hz reduces flicker and possible eyestrain.

LCD monitors do not have flicker problems or the same range of adjustable refresh rates as CRTs, so these can be left at the Windows default settings.

Adjusting your resolution and refresh rate may alter the size of the display on your monitor.

If this happens, you can use the monitor's controls to adjust the display so that it fits the screen. Usually, this is achieved using buttons just below the monitor's screen area. The specific steps you take to achieve this will depend on the manufacturer of the monitor. You should consult the manual for instructions on resizing the display.

Other peripheral devices

Connecting an overhead projector

The following are general guidelines and will vary according to the computer and overhead projector you are using. When attaching an overhead projector to a computer, you should consult the manuals for both devices.

First, ensure the power is switched off on all devices, and that they are plugged out of the electrical supply.

Place the projector where you will want it, then try to arrange other devices around it.

Find the correct socket to insert the connector cable between the computer and the projector. Plug this into both devices and tighten the thumbscrews to ensure the connection is secure.

Connect any other peripheral devices to the computer, mouse, keyboard, controllers, etc. Plug in the devices and switch them on.

The projector should detect the computer and project whatever is on the screen onto a wall or screen. Despite the range of computers and projectors available, most of these devices are now designed to work together seamlessly.

If the projector does not sense the display signal from your computer, you will have to perform one of two actions:

Specifically with laptops, you may need to press a number of keys to send the signal to the projector. Many laptops now include a function button, which is coloured blue and has 'Fn' printed in a square on it. You often press this button along with one of the function keys (F1 – F12) to send the display signal to the projector. You should refer to the computer manual to find the specific keys you need to use.

Alternatively, you may need to install the projector for the computer. The *Found New Hardware Wizard* should display on your computer, and follow the instructions to install the projector. You may need the CD that contains the drivers for the projector.

Install a modem

How you install a modem for a computer will depend on the type of modem you have. Many modems plug directly into a USB port and are Plug and Play ready. Others have to be added to the computer's motherboard.

The majority of modern modems are compatible with Plug and Play technology. This means that once they are physically installed according to the manufacturer's instructions, Windows should automatically install the software that will allow them to work.

If you want to install a modem internally, you should check the warranty and/or guarantee information for the computer. Many manufacturers will void any warranties or guarantees if you remove the casing of a computer yourself. They may require you to take the computer to a specialist or one of their agents. If this is not the case, you can install an internal modem using the following steps.

1. Switch off the computer and unplug it from the power supply.

2. Remove the casing.

3. Locate the PCI expansion slot on the motherboard.

4. Connect the modem into the slot. Ensure the connection is secure.

5. Replace the computer casing.

6. Start the computer.

For an external modem, you plug the modem into the appropriate port on the computer. This may be a SCSI port or, more often, a USB port.

Once the modem has been attached to the computer, switch on your computer to install it.

When the computer starts up, the *Found New Hardware Wizard* may run. If this happens, click *Next* to install the modem. You may need to identify a location for the modem drivers, for example, on a CD or location on the computer.

If the *Found New Hardware Wizard* does not start, use the following steps to complete the installation:

Actions

▸ 1. Click *Start*, select *Control Panel*.

▸ 2. Click *Phone and Modem Options*.

▸ 3. Click the *Modems* tab.

Actions

▸ 4. Select the modem and the computer now downloads the driver code to support the new hardware. Click *Next*.

▸ 5. Click *OK*.

If the modem you connected is not listed in the *Modems* tab, click the *Add* button to install the drivers for it. This will open the *Install New Modem* dialogue box. Click *Next* to start the process.

Most modems today come pre-installed in newly purchased computers.

Installing RAM

Windows should detect any new device you install in your system. One of the most useful additions to a computer is installing extra RAM.

Installing RAM significantly improves the performance of a computer. You may need to install RAM if a computer starts to slow down, or if it is required by a piece of hardware or software you want to install. If you are buying RAM, you need to make sure it is compatible the your make and model of computer. You may be able to find this information from the computer's manual or the RAM manufacturer.

As with modems, you should consult any warranty and guarantee information as well as your manual before installing RAM. You will need to remove the casing of the computer, which could void a warranty or guarantee. Some manufacturers will ask you to bring the computer to an expert or one of their agents to add RAM for you.

If this is not the case, you can install the RAM yourself. Switch off the computer and unplug it. Wait a minute or so before doing anything else. This gives time for any electrical current or signals to discharge.

Remove the casing from the computer. You should use insulated tools when doing this to prevent electrical shock.

While working inside the case, be mindful of static electricity. To avoid building up a static charge that could potentially short out a component, some people use an anti-static strap to ground themselves (available from most computer hardware retailers).

Locate the RAM sockets on the motherboard. Most computers have two RAM sockets, many have up to four.

You should refer to the computer manual for RAM installation instructions. For many computers, the following method is used. However, this may not be the case with the specific make and model you are using.

At either end of the RAM socket, there will be retaining clips. Push these outward to open them up. Slot the RAM into the socket. You should not need to force it.

Once the RAM is securely in place, replace the computer's cover. Plug in the computer and switch it on.

With the RAM securely fastened replace the computer's side panel and screw it into place. Plug in the power supply unit (remembering to flip the switch back on) and boot up.

The add hardware wizard

If Windows does not detect a newly connected device, use the *Add Hardware Wizard* to get the device recognised and the drivers installed.

You can increase the functionality of your basic computer by adding hardware devices not supplied with your initial configuration. You may add external peripherals such as scanners, CD drives, or other storage devices or you may add internal interface cards such as sound cards or network cards. These can be added following the supplier's instructions or using the *Add Hardware Wizard*.

The *Add Hardware Wizard* will guide you through the process of installing the drivers for new hardware. You should only need to use this if Windows does not recognise the hardware you have attached or installed.

Use the following steps to open the *Add Hardware Wizard*:

Action

▶ 1. Click *Start*, select *Control Panel*.

▶ 2. Click *Add Hardware*, the *Add Hardware Wizard* dialogue box displays, click *Next*.

The *Add Hardware Wizard* will then search for new hardware attached to the computer. If the hardware is found, and an appropriate driver is already on the operating system, Windows will install the hardware automatically.

If the Wizard cannot find the hardware, a message is displayed, asking you to confirm that the hardware is connected. Make sure the device is connected to the computer. Then enable the *Yes* option and click *Next*.

A list of hardware attached to the computer is displayed. If your hardware is in the list, select it and click *Next*. If the hardware is not displayed in the list, scroll to the bottom of the dialogue box and select the *Add a new hardware device* option, then click *Next*.

Click *Next* on the *Welcome Screen*, and the Wizard will search for hardware that has been connected but does not yet have a driver installed.

If it detects the device, select it, and the Wizard will install the driver. If it does not detect the device, it will ask you if the hardware is connected. When you answer *Yes* and click *Next*, it will give you a list of installed hardware.

If the device is in the list, select it and then click *Next*. If not, scroll to the bottom and select *Add a new hardware device*, and then click *Next*.

If the device is a printer, network card or modem select *Search for and Install hardware automatically* and click *Next*. Once it detects the device and installs the driver the task is complete and the driver is installed.

If the device is a printer, network card or modem select *Search for and Install hardware automatically* and click *Next*. Once it detects the device and installs the driver the task is complete and the driver is installed.

 In Windows Vista, the *Add Hardware Wizard* can be accessed in *Control Panel*, classic view. A similar installation process is used.

Installing plug and play devices

> Plug and Play, sometimes, abbreviated PnP, is a phrase used to describe devices that work with a computer system as soon as they are connected.

Plug and Play describes hardware that will start working almost immediately after being plugged into a computer. Either the device itself, or the computer will have all the necessary drivers.

As an example, a Plug and Play mouse can be connected to the USB port of a computer and start working in seconds. A non-Plug and Play device would require you to use the *Add New Hardware Wizard* to install the drivers required before you could use the mouse.

Plug and Play usually refers to peripheral devices, such as keyboards, mice and external drives. However, some internal hardware can also be Plug and Play. A simple example of this is a video card. These are often recognised as soon as they are installed. However, because they need to be installed within the computer casing, the computer must be turned off when installing the card. External devices can usually be attached while the computer is running. For example, if you connect a Plug and Play mouse to the USB port on your computer, it will begin to work within a few seconds of being plugged in.

While Plug and Play usually refers to computer peripheral devices, such as keyboards and mice, it can also be used to describe internal hardware. For example, a video card or hard drive may be a Plug-and-Play device, meaning the computer will recognise it as soon as it is installed.

Adding assistive technology

> Assistive Technology (AT) is the name given to hardware and software that helps people with disabilities interact more easily with a computer.

It is vital that any Assistive Technology you add to a computer is compatible with the computer's OS, hardware and applications.

The assistive technology products available include the following:

- *Alternative keyboards:* featuring larger or smaller than standard keys or keyboards, alternative key configurations, and keyboards for use with one hand.

- *Electronic pointing devices:* used to control the cursor on the screen without use of hands. Devices used include ultrasound, infrared beams, eye movements, nerve signals, or brain waves.

- *Sip-and-puff systems:* activated by inhaling or exhaling.

- *Wands and sticks:* worn on the head, held in the mouth or strapped to the chin and used to press keys on the keyboard.

- *Joysticks:* manipulated by hand, feet, chin, etc and used to control the cursor on screen.

- *Trackballs:* movable balls on top of a base that can be used to move the cursor on screen.

- *Touch screens*: allow direct selection or activation of the computer by touching the screen, making it easier to select an option directly rather than through a mouse movement or keyboard. Touch screens are either built into the computer monitor or can be added onto a computer monitor.

- *Braille embossers*: these transfer computer generated text into embossed Braille output. Braille translation programs convert text scanned-in or generated via standard word processing programs into Braille, which can then be printed on the embosser.

- *Keyboard filters*: are typing aids such as word prediction utilities and add-on spelling checkers that reduce the required number of keystrokes. Keyboard filters enable users to quickly access the letters they need and to avoid inadvertently selecting keys they don't want.

- *On-screen keyboards*: provide an image of a standard or modified keyboard on the computer screen. This allows the user to select keys with a mouse, touch screen, trackball, joystick, switch, or electronic pointing device. On-screen keyboards often have a scanning option that highlights individual keys that can be selected by the user. On-screen keyboards are helpful for individuals who are not able to use a standard keyboard due to dexterity or mobility difficulties.

- *Speech recognition or voice recognition programs*: allow people to give commands and enter data using their voices rather than a mouse or keyboard. Voice recognition systems use a microphone attached to the computer, which can be used to create text documents such as letters or email messages, browse the Internet, and navigate among applications and menus by voice.

- *Talking and large-print word processors*: are software programs that use speech synthesisers to provide auditory feedback of what is typed. Large-print word processors allow the user to view everything in large text without added screen enlargement.

- *Text-to-Speech (TTS) or speech synthesisers screen reader software*: receive information going to the screen in the form of letters, numbers, and punctuation marks, and then 'speak' it out loud in a computerised voice. Using speech synthesisers allows computer users who are blind or who have learning difficulties to hear what they are typing and also provide a spoken voice for individuals who can not communicate orally, but can communicate their thoughts through typing.

Both Vista and XP contain many built in accessibility features.

Cleaning peripherals and storage media

It is good practice to clean the computer, components, peripherals and storage media like CDs and DVDs regularly. This will help to keep the computers in good working order and prolong its life. The following are some categories which should be addressed as part of an organisation's policy as regards computer maintenance policy.

General cleaning tips

It is good practice to follow these tips when cleaning a computer, components, peripherals or storage media:

- Always switch off and disconnect any electrical device before cleaning it.

- Never spray a cleaning agent directly onto what you are cleaning. Spray the liquid onto a cloth or tissue and use that to clean the item.

- When using cleaning agents, wear gloves and take extra care not to spill them in the area you are using them. Avoid skin contact and inhaling fumes.

- A mini vacuum is a useful way to remove dust that builds up on the outside of electrical devices. However, never use a vacuum on internal components.

- Never use compressed air to clean computer parts.

- When cleaning fans inside a device, use something to prevent the fan blades from moving.

- Forbid eating, drinking or smoking near computers.

Case cleaning

Keeping the casing of computers and other devices clean improves their appearance, but can also help to extend the life of the device. A build up of dust or dirt can clog ventilation holes, which can cause computer or other devices to build up heat within them.

Rub the casing with a damp, lint free cloth. Use a small amount of cleaning agent to remove difficult stains. Check ventilation holes, ports and drives are free of hair or lint.

Cleaning CD/DVD drives

CD/DVD drives need to be kept clean to avoid read errors or damage to discs.

There are a variety of CD/DVD drive cleaners available. These often include a disc with a small line of brushes on it. You should buy a reliable one and follow the instructions for its use.

Some people also wipe the drive tray with a damp cloth. If you do this, make sure it is completely dry before the tray goes back into the drive.

CD / DVD disc cleaning

Dirty CDs and DVDs can quickly become unreadable, which can cause a loss of information and/or prevent installation of software saved on the disc.

There is a range of CD/DVD cleaning kits available. You should buy a reliable one and follow the instructions for its use carefully. Improper use of these cleaning kits or trying to clean discs with a cloth can cause damage or scratches to the CD/DVD.

Keyboard cleaning

Dust, hair, dirt and food particles can build up on and between the keys of a keyboard. This presents a health risk, as it spreads germs. But the physical debris can also break your keyboard or make it unresponsive.

Switch off the computer and disconnect the keyboard. Hold the keyboard upside down and use a lint free cloth, slightly damp with disinfectant to remove dust and other dirt build up on the keys.

If liquid spills onto the keyboard, disconnect it immediately and try to dry it out. In these cases, it might be a better idea to just replace the keyboard.

Monitor cleaning

Dirt and dust on a monitor can be unsightly and make it harder to read the information displayed.

Before cleaning a monitor, you should ensure it is switched off and unplugged from any electrical source.

Special cleaning wipes for monitors are widely available. You should buy and use these, following the manufacturers guidelines for use.

For monitors with an antiglare coating, you can use a lightly dampened cloth to wipe off any dust. Using a cleaning agent or harsh chemical could remove or destroy the antiglare coating.

Mouse cleaning

Dirt and dust in the mechanism of a mouse can cause it to become unresponsive or unpredictable. How you clean your mouse will depend on whether it has a ball or not.

If the mouse does have a ball in it, turn it upside down and turn the access cover counter clockwise for about a quarter of an inch. The cover should pop out a little, allowing you to take it off and remove the ball. Clean around the wheels with a lightly damp, lint free cloth. Also clean the ball and the access cover. Then, reinsert the ball and screw the access cover back on.

Printer cleaning

Dirt building up on a printer looks unsightly and can spread germs. Switch off the printer and unplug it before cleaning it. Use a lightly damp cloth with a little antibacterial agent to rub the dirt off the surface of the printer. If the inside of the printer needs cleaning, you should refer to the printer manual for instructions on how to do this.

Scanner cleaning

Dirt and dust on a scanner can look unsightly and spread germs. If dust builds up on the inside of a scanner, it will affect the quality of scanned documents. To clean the outside of the scanner, a lightly damp cloth with a little disinfectant will remove most dust and dirt. You should refer to the scanner manual for instructions on cleaning the inside.

Software

Introduction

Software tools help people communicate, collaborate and improve productivity. This section explains how to obtain, download and install software for computers. Downloading software is gaining popularity, as Internet connection speeds increase, making it quick and easy to download and install a piece of software as you need it.

You should always research any piece of software you are downloading by checking reviews from users and industry experts.

One website that will help you identify the right software is www.download.com. This website provides descriptions and reviews of an extensive range of software, as well as links to download the software. Some of this software is free, others are commercial products.

Thunderbird

Thunderbird is an open source email application developed by the Mozilla Foundation. This application has many of the features of other popular email clients, such as Microsoft's Outlook Express, but is free to download and programmers can modify the software itself, so that it can be customised to meet their needs.

Use the following steps to download Thunderbird:

Thunderbird™ 2

Mozilla's Thunderbird 2 email application is more powerful than ever. It's now even easier to organize, secure and customize your mail.

Download Thunderbird
2.0.0.12 for Windows, English
(US) (6.4MB)

Actions

▸ 1. Open a web browser and go to the following address: http://www.mozillamessaging.com/en-US/thunderbird/

▸ 2. Click *Download Thunderbird*.

▸ 3. A dialogue box will ask what you want to do. Click *Save File*.

▶ 4. Once the file has downloaded, double-click on it to run it. Then click *Run* when asked.

▶ 5. Click *Next* in the setup page to begin installing Thunderbird. You will have to agree to the Software License Agreement to install the software. To do this enable the *I accept the terms in the license agreement* option and click *Next* and complete the instructions.

Installing the Firefox browser

Internet Explorer is installed with all computers that run Microsoft Windows operating systems, so most computers will have an Internet browser on it.

New versions of Internet Explorer and other browsers can be downloaded and used. Different browsers offer a range of features that will suit different users. Whichever browser is used, it is good practice and will improve browsing experience to keep the browser updated, and this should be part of the maintenance policy for software.

For the purposes of demonstration, this Course Book outlines the steps you take to download and install the Firefox browser. However, the procedure will be similar for any browser.

Use the following steps to download Firefox:

▶ 1. Open a web browser and go to the following address: http://www.mozilla.com/firefox/

▶ 2. Click *Free Download*,

▶ 3. A dialogue box will ask what you want to do. Click *Save File*.

Double-click on the file you downloaded to launch the setup application. The Firefox installation process is very similar to that of installing Thunderbird. Click *Next* until the application is installed, then click *Finish*. You also have the option of opening Firefox immediately after closing the setup application.

Installing utility software

Utility software helps with the running of your computer. By way of example, two types of utility software are discussed in this section: diagnostic software and antivirus software.

Diagnostic software

Diagnostic software will examine how a computer is running and identify potential problems or conflicts within the computer.

This type of application is used to identify and report the cause of a problem on a computer. This is a useful tool to have, as it may help you speed up the troubleshooting process. There is a wide range of diagnostic software available, which can be downloaded from the Internet.

A good place to look for a diagnostic utility software is the following website:
http://download.cnet.com/windows/diagnostic-software/

You can identify the type of diagnostic utility you require by reviewing what they do and how easy other users found the software to work with.

Download antivirus software

Every computer should have antivirus software installed on it. Even if the computer does not have an Internet connection, malicious software can infect a computer through USB keys or CDs and DVDs. Antivirus software can be bought on CD or downloaded from the Internet. As with any software, it is a necessary good idea to thoroughly research the antivirus software you intend to use.

Many computers sold with an operating system installed will also include a trial version of antivirus software. You should check reviews of this software and identify whether you want to keep it, or use another application. If you decide to use another application, you should install that application before uninstalling the antivirus software already on the computer.

When first installed, many antivirus applications will first update their own databases and check for any upgrades. It is good practice to allow the application to do this.

You will then be asked where the antivirus should check for updates. When given the choice, most people select *Internet*. Some antivirus applications will not give you a choice, they will only accept updates from the Internet.

You can specify a location on the network for computers to check for updates. This helps to reduce Internet bandwidth as you can download the updates on one machine, but then allow other computers to access it to get updates. Whichever option you decide on, it is vital that your antivirus software can check and update itself at least once a day.

When installing antivirus software for the first time, you may need to adjust your firewall settings so that the antivirus update can access the Internet and download any updates.

You should also run a virus scan and set a schedule for the software to run a regular scan on all computers.

Installing software

Buying and installing software using a CD/DVD is still very common. Many people like the benefit of having a full package with installation instructions, and covers so they can store the software for use again. With downloaded software, you have to organise this yourself.

Most software CDs will launch themselves when you insert the CD in the drive. An installation application will then guide you through the installation process.

If a CD does not launch automatically, you can use the following steps to install the software:

Actions

▶ 1. Click *Start*, select *Control Panel*.

▶ 2. Click *Add or Remove Programs*.

▶ 3. Click *Add new program* in the left pane.

▶ 4. Click *CD or Floppy* to identify where the installation file is.

Windows will then find the installation file and launch it.

Removing software

Most applications have an Uninstall utility that you can use to remove the application and any other items which the installation process may have created, for example, shortcuts to launch an application. If an application does not have an Uninstall utility, you can use the *Add or Remove programs* utility in Windows.

Actions

▶ 1. Click *Start*, select *Control Panel*.

▶ 2. Double-click *Add or Remove Programs*.

▶ 3. Click *Change or Remove Programs*.

▶ 4. Click on the application you want to remove.

▶ 5. Click *Change/Remove*.

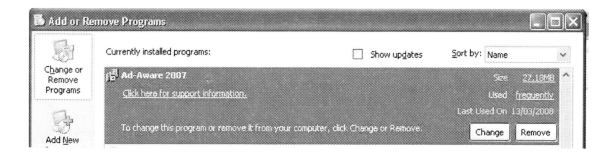

Quick Quiz

Select the correct answer from the following multiple-choice questions:

I   Insert the missing words, to complete the sentence from the options below:

A _____ _____type of printer produces characters and illustrations by striking pins against an ink ribbon to print closely spaced dots in the appropriate shape.

a   Dot matrix

b   Laser jet

c   Daisy wheel

d   Inkjet

2   If, while printing you notice that lines are uneven, what should you do?

a   Update the printer driver

b   Manually clean the printer

c   Change the ink cartridge

d   Align the print heads

3   How should you correct a CRT monitor that has a flickering screen causing you eyestrain?

a   Check the video card is installed correctly

b   Use display to change the screen size

c   Change the monitor case

d   Change the refresh rate to 72 Hz or 75 Hz

4   What type of Assistive technology device is described in the following statement?

An accessibility utility that displays a virtual keyboard on the computer screen that allows people with disability impairments to type data by using a pointing device or joystick.

a   Touch screen

b   On-screen keyboard

c   Keyboard filters

d   Speech recognition

Answers to Quick Quiz

1   a   Dot matrix

2   d   Align the print heads

3   d   Change the refresh rate to 72 Hz or 75 Hz

4   b   On-screen keyboard

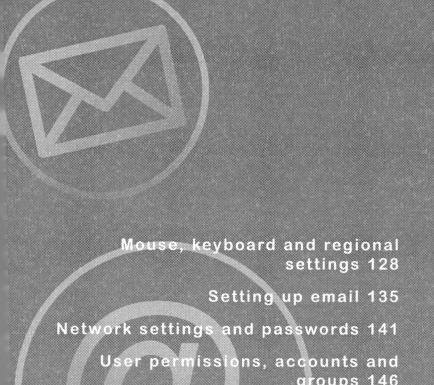

Admin

Concepts

Connect

Operating system

Install

Admin

Measuring points

- Change mouse, keyboard settings
- Change regional settings, language settings
- Be able to add or remove fonts etc
- Adjust accessibility settings
- Configure email software
- Install and setup a simple mail server setup
- Set up email accounts, webmail accounts
- Understand and configure different network protocols
- Set up a new user group
- Modify permissions for a user or for a user group
- Add, remove users to/from a group

- Install, configure and remove network services
- Access usage details, user details, logon time, passwords, memberships etc
- Create common resources, files, printers
- Troubleshoot user access/permissions issues
- Know about good password policies
- Understand the term virus and the main virus types: Trojan horses, viruses, worms etc
- Be aware of various laws and guidelines that are applicable.

Introduction

There is significant loss of productivity when computers or networks are not functioning optimally.

This chapter deals with a range of administrative tasks and settings which can be applied to improve interaction with computers for users. This includes adjusting hardware to make it easier to use, setting up email, network settings and permissions and understanding the importance of using antivirus software to protect your network and the computers on it from malicious software.

Mouse, keyboard and regional settings

This section deals with adjusting a range of hardware and computer settings to optimise the computer's use.

Customising a mouse

The mouse settings on a computer are designed to meet the needs of most users. However, you can change a range of settings so that it works better for a specific user. Some typical changes are to define the speed of clicks for a double-click and changing the pointer image.

Use the following steps to open the *Mouse Properties* dialogue box, where you can adjust its settings:

> **Actions**
>
> ▶ 1. Click *Start*, select *Control Panel*.
>
> ▶ 2. Select *Mouse*.

Changing the speed with which a user has to click for the computer to register a double-click is a common setting that people change. In the *Mouse Properties* dialogue box, you can use the following steps to define the double-click speed for a mouse:

Double-click speed

Double-click the folder to test your setting. If the folder does not open or close, try using a slower setting.

Speed: Slow ————◻———— Fast

> **Actions**
>
> ▶ 1. Click *Buttons*.
>
> ▶ 2. Drag the *Double-click speed* slider to the left to make it slower and to the right to make it faster.
>
> ▶ 3. Test the speed by clicking the test icon.
>
> ▶ 4. Click *Apply* to save your changes.

Changing the mouse pointer can make it more attractive, but it can also make it easier to use. A typical example is where a user uses a larger pointer to make it easier to see on the screen.

In the *Mouse Properties* dialogue box, click *Pointers* and choose your requirements under *Customize*.

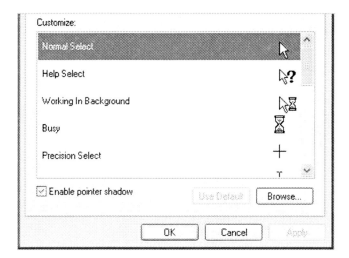

Select a pointer style from the *Scheme* drop down. This will display samples of how the pointer is displayed during specific events (for example, how the pointer looks normally, or when the computer is busy, or on other events). There is a range of larger schemes for those who have difficulty seeing the pointer. When you have decided on a pointer scheme to use, click *Apply* to save your changes.

Click the *Pointer Options* tab for some other useful settings, including:

- *Select a pointer speed:* defines how fast the pointer moves across the screen.

- *Automatically move pointer to the deafult button in a dialogue box.* This can save time.

- *Display pointer trails:* shows visual echo of the pointer's path as it moves across the screen.

- *Show location of pointer when I press the CTRL: key* if enabled, the mouse is highlighted on the screen when the control button is pressed on a keyboard.

Click *Apply* to save any changes you make, and click *OK* to exit

Click *OK* at the bottom of the dialogue box to close the *Mouse Properties*.

Changing regional settings

Windows can be displayed in over 100 languages and dialects. Allowing people to interact with a computer in their own language helps to improve productivity, as they do not need to translate everything they are reading as they work.

You can switch between languages, or even define a specific language for each user on a computer. To do this, you will need to first add your preferred languages. You can do this from the *Regional and Language Options* dialogue box:

Regional and
Language
Options

Actions

▶ 1. Click *Start*, select *Settings* and *Control Panel*.

▶ 2. Click *Regional and Language Options*.

In the *Regional and Language Options* dialogue box for Microsoft XP:

Actions

▶ 3. Click the *Languages* tab and click *Details*.

▶ 4. Click *Add* and select an input language and keyboard layout from the displayed drop down lists.

▶ 5. Click *OK*.

English is the default language for Windows. Any other languages you require will need to be installed. Language packs can be downloaded from www.microsoft.com

If you have more than one language installed on the computer, you need to let Windows know which language should be default.

In the *Text services and input languages* dialogue box, select the language from the *Default input language* drop down and click *OK*. The languages selected will display when the computer starts.

In the *Languages* tab, you can install language files for:

• Inputting and displaying complex scripts and supporting right to left text input.

• East Asian languages

To switch between languages

If more than one language is installed on a computer, Windows XP displays the *Language Bar* in the lower-right corner, near the system clock. To give an example, for English language computers, the letters EN are displayed.

Accessibility settings

Windows has a range of accessibility settings that are intended to help people with disabilities to use their computers more productively.

Use the following steps to open *Windows Accessibility* options:

Accessibility
Options

Actions

▸ 1. Click *Start*, select *Control Panel*.

▸ 2. Click *Accessibility options* in XP.

- In Vista, this is called *Ease of Access Center*.

This opens the *Accessibility Options* (or *Ease of Access Centre* in Vista). In this dialogue box, there is a range of features you can use to activate different accessibility options.

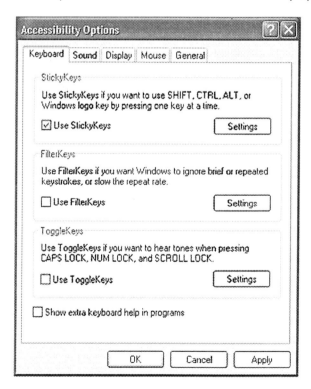

The 'Keyboard' tab

There is a range of accessibility features you can enable to make using a keyboard easier. These include StickyKeys, FilterKeys and ToggleKeys. These can be enabled or disabled by clicking, or clearing, the checkbox beside each.

StickyKeys: will allow users who may not be able to hold down two keys at one time, for example to use the *Ctrl* and *S* shortcut to save a document. With StickyKeys enabled, the user can press the *Ctrl* key, then the *S* key to achieve the same outcome.

FilterKeys: will adjust the keyboard response, to prevent a letter being repeated when a key is inadvertently pressed more than once in quick succession. It can also be used to prevent the letter being repeated when the key is held down for an extended period of time.

ToggleKeys: will play a sound when either the NUMLOCK, CAPS LOCK or SCROLL LOCK are turned on or off. A high pitch sound is played when they are switched on, a low pitch sound is played when they are switched off.

The sounds tab

Windows also offers a range of sound options to help those who may have difficulty hearing or working with system sounds on the computer for example, warning sounds. These options are known as *SoundSentry* and *ShowSounds*:

SoundSentry: will display visual warnings whenever the computer generates a sound, for example, the title bar may blink. This alerts users to standard system issues that may occur.

ShowSounds: instructs applications that usually provide information using sounds to provide a caption or icon instead.

To turn on these accessibility features click the required check box in the *Sound* tab.

The display tab

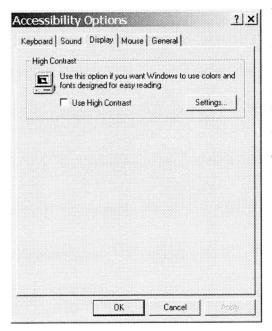

The *Display* tab allows you to turn on or off the *High Contrast* option. *High Contrast* is an accessibility feature designed for people who have vision impairment. High Contrast colour schemes can increase legibility for some users by heightening screen contrast with alternative colour combinations. Some of the schemes also change font sizes for greater legibility.

There are other accessibility features available within *Accessibility Options*. These can be found in the *Mouse* tab and *General* tab.

Fonts

A font defines the shape and characteristics of the text displayed on your computer.

Microsoft Windows includes different types of fonts, for example:

- Verdana (TrueType)
- MS Serif
- MS Sans Serif
- Arial (TrueType)
- Times New Roman (TrueType)
- Symbol (Symbol) (TrueType)

If you want to add new fonts in Windows, these new fonts must be TrueType fonts (Font Standard) or particularly designed for Windows.

Adding fonts

Use the following steps to install new fonts on a computer:

> **Actions**
>
> ▶ 1. Click *Start*, select *Control Panel*.
>
> ▶ 2. Click *Fonts*.
>
> ▶ 3. Click *File*, select *Install New Font*.
>
> ▶ 4. Browse to the location of your new fonts
>
> - This could be a drive, folder, CD/DVD or network location.
>
> ▶ 5. Click the font you want to add.
>
> ▶ 6. Repeat this process to add as many fonts as you want.
>
> ▶ 7. Enable the *Copy fonts to Fonts folder* option.
>
> ▶ 8. Click *OK*.

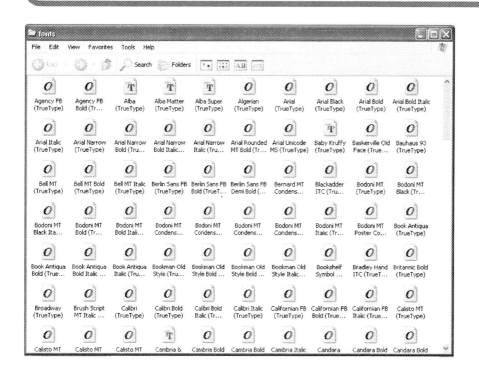

Removing fonts

You would not normally need to remove a font from a computer. However you can use the following steps to do so:

> **Actions**
>
> ▶ 1. Click the font you want to remove.
>
>   • You can click more than one by holding down the *Ctrl* key while clicking the mouse.
>
> ▶ 2. Right-click over one of the selected fonts and click *Delete*.
>
> ▶ 3. Click *OK* to confirm deletion.

Setting up email

Email has become one of the most powerful communication tools for people and organisations across the world, as it helps people communicate, collaborate and share information. This section outlines how you should set up an email application. In this case, Microsoft Outlook is used to send and receive email from your organisation's email addresses. Setting up a webmail account is also covered and Gmail is used as an example here.

Configuring email applications

The instructions outlined in this section can be used to set up an email client (specifically, Microsoft Outlook) on a computer. The procedure outlined will be similar for any email client you may want to configure.

Before setting up an email application to send and receive email, the account must be set up on the email server. The email server is where emails are sent to and stored before being downloaded by a computer.

This requires:

• Ensuring email hosting is enabled for your domain.

• A mailbox has been set up for the account you want to configure on the computer.

If you are unsure whether your email hosting has been set up, you should contact your ISP.

To set up an email application, you will need to know details for:

• Your incoming mail server (usually a POP3 server).

• Your outgoing mail server (usually an SMTP server).

POP3 stands for Post Office Protocol 3, which is used to collect email from a mail server. SMTP stands for Simple Mail Transfer Protocol. This is used to send email to a server, which will then send it to its intended recipient.

Your incoming and outgoing mail servers may not necessarily be POP3 and SMTP, but these are the most widely used standards. You should contact your network administrator or ISP for the details of your email accounts, so that you can set up the email application to send and receive email for them.

This section outlines the steps you take to do this. For the purposes of demonstration, the steps outlined here refer to Microsoft's Outlook application. However, many email applications have similar menu commands.

To add a new email account, carry out the following steps:

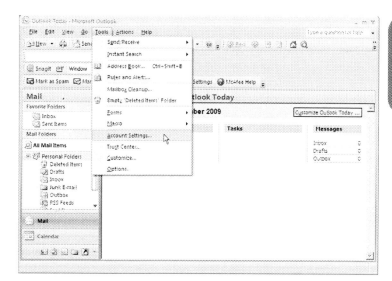

Action

▶ 1. In *Outlook*, select *Tools*, and click on *Account Settings*.

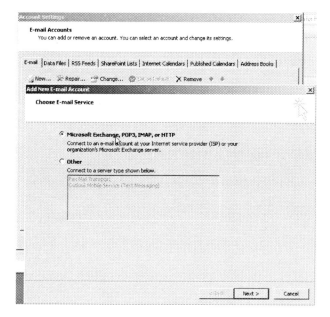

Action

▶ 2. Click on the 'View' icon to add a new e-mail contact.

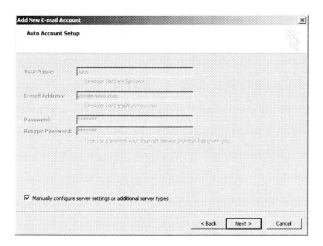

Action

▶ 3. In the next screen, provide details for the email account you are adding. You will need to add:

- Name

- Email address

- Password information

▶ 4. Click the check box in the bottom left-hand corner to manually configure server settings.

▶ 5. Choose the kind of e-mail account required.

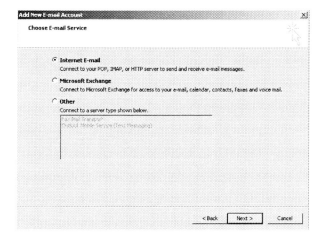

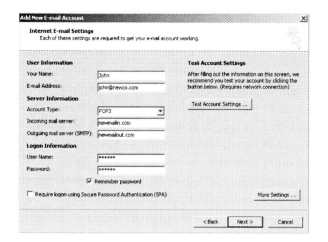

▶ 6. Add your server information including incoming and outgoing mail server details (these details will be provided to you by your ISP).

▶ 7. Click the *Test Account Settings* button to check that the information you have entered is correct. This will let you know if the server information, email address and login information is correct for the account.

Select *Secure Password Authentication (SPA)* check box only if your server requires authentication. Discuss this with your ISP as this functionality will vary from ISP to ISP.

Actions

▶ 8. There are other settings you may need to specify for your email account. Click the *More Settings* button to view these. This will open settings under four tabs where you can:

- *General*: specify the organisation you work for.

- *Outgoing server*: define whether your SMTP server requires authentication (you will be told if this is the case). If you are unsure, contact your ISP.

- *Connection*: define how the computer should contact the email server (for example, over dialup, through the network).

- *Advanced*: define more specific options related to your mail server. You should not change these values unless instructed by your ISP.

You do not normally need to make changes in the *More Settings* dialogue box.

▶ 9. Once you have added all your information in *E-mail Settings*, click *Next*. Click *Finish* to complete the setup process.

Setting up webmail accounts

Webmail has increased in popularity as organisations can now collect email from their own servers through webmail accounts. This means people can collect and send email wherever they are, without having to have a specific computer with them.

Two popular webmail accounts are Hotmail from Microsoft and Gmail from Google. For the purposes of demonstration, setting up a Gmail account is covered here. However, many webmail services will use similar steps to create accounts.

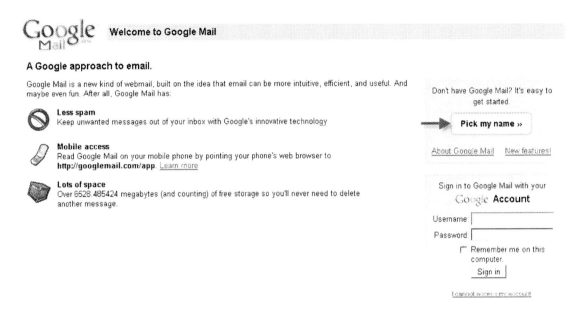

To create a Gmail account:

Actions

▸ 1. Access the link www.mail.google.com/

▸ 2. Click *Sign up for Gmail.*

▸ 3. Complete the fields in the form to sign up.

You will need to complete a sign up form and include details such as your name, preferred email address and password. You may need to try a few times to get an email address that is not already in use.

Below is a sample selection of a sign up form.

Your Google Account gives you access to Google Mail and other Google services. If you already have a Google Account, you can sign in here.

Get started with Google Mail

First name:

Last name:

Desired Login Name: @googlemail.com

Examples: JSmith, John Smith

check availability!

Choose a password: Password strength:

Minimum of 8 characters in length.

Re-enter password:

☑ Remember me on this computer.

Creating a Google Account will enable Web History. Web History is a feature that will provide you with a more personalized experience on Google that includes more relevant search results and recommendations. Learn More

☑ Enable Web History.

Security Question: Choose a question ...

If you forget your password we will ask for the answer to your security question. Learn More

Answer:

Secondary email:

This address is used to authenticate your account should you ever encounter problems or forget your password. If you do not have another email address, you may leave this field blank. Learn More

Your organisation may wish to set its own policy about how web based email accounts are used.

Network settings and passwords

This section outlines the process for configuring your network so that the computers and devices on it can communicate with others. Protecting security by implementing a good password policy will also be dealt with.

Configuring network protocols

Network protocols and services are what make communication between computers possible. Information is sent around networks in packets that need to be put back together in order to be read.

When communicating within a network, it is important that:

- Computers or other devices prepare information in a way that other devices can read it.

- Information is sent in such a way that when it is received, the recipient knows what it is and how to put it together.

- Each device knows where to pass information so that it can reach its intended recipient.

- Information from several computers or devices can be dealt with appropriately without losing (or dropping) information.

Network protocols and services are the languages, rules and codes that make these possible. All networks have some kind of protocol. But TCP / IP is probably the most widespread.

Configuring TCP / IP

> TCP / IP is a suite of protocols used by the Internet to communicate exchange and share information between devices.

As a standard, it has become very popular. Many networks that are connected to the Internet use the TCP / IP protocol suite to enable devices to communicate with each other.

The TCP / IP settings for a computer can only be configured by an administrator, or someone with administrator privileges.

To add a computer to a network:

Actions

▶ 1. Click *Start*, select *Control Panel*.

▶ 2. Double-click *System*.

▶ 3. Click *Computer Name*.

▶ 4. Type a brief description for the computer in the *Computer Description* field.

▶ 5. Click *Change* button.

▶ 6. Type the computer name in the *Computer Name* field.

Actions

▶ 7. Enable the *Workgroup* option and type a workgroup name into the field.

▶ 8. Click *OK* to save the computer name and workgroup changes.

▶ 9. Click *OK* to exit the *System Properties* dialogue box.

Next, you need to set up the computer's network connection:

Actions

▶ 1. Click *Start*, select *Control Panel*, select *Network Connections*.

▶ 2. Select *Local Area Connection* and right-click *Properties*.

▶ 3. Click *General*.

▶ 4. Enable the *Client for Microsoft Networks* option.

▶ 5. Click *Properties*, just under the list.

▶ 6. Select *Windows Locator* from the *Name Service Provider* drop down list.

▶ 7. Click *OK*.

Finally, you need to check the TCP / IP settings to ensure the computer will be able to communicate with devices on the network. Use the following steps to do this:

Actions

▶ 1. Enable the *Internet Protocol (TCP / IP)* option.

　　● If this option is not displayed, you can install it by clicking *Install*, selecting *Protocol* and selecting *TCP / IP*.

▶ 2. With *Internet Properties* (TCP / IP) highlighted, click *Properties*.

▶ 3. Enable the *Obtain an IP address automatically* option.

▶ 4. Enable the *Obtain DNS server addresses automatically* option.

▶ 5. Click *OK* to exit the *TCP / IP Properties* dialogue box.

▶ 6. Click *OK* to exit the *Local Area Connection Properties* dialogue box.

Password policies

Username and password combinations are still the most popular form of authentication. This section discusses the problems with password authentication and some strategies for overcoming these problems.

> A password is a specific series of characters used in conjunction with a username to authenticate an individual.

A password can be compromised in a number of ways. Typical examples include:

- Writing down or sharing the password with others.

- Using simple passwords that can be easily guessed by people or applications.

- Transmitting passwords without an appropriate level of encryption.

- Saving a password on a computer or network without an appropriate level of security.

- Resetting a password for someone without proper authentication.

A compromised password will cause serious problems for the security of information stored on computers or servers in your network. Someone who has access to another's password can pose as that person on the system. This threatens the confidentiality, integrity and availability of information on the system.

Password security is a very important issue for any organisation. However, one of the main barriers to implementing a highly secure password policy is user limitation. It is important to remember when developing a password management system that users are only human. Specifically, it can be hard for people to remember:

- Complicated passwords.

- Passwords for different systems.

- Passwords that change frequently.

- Passwords that they do not use regularly.

If someone has trouble remembering their password, they will generally do one (or more) of the following:

- Write down their password, compromising its security.

- Forget their password, causing access problems and/or requiring frequent assistance from the helpdesk.

- Use very simple passwords that might be guessed.

- Reuse a single password as often as possible.

You should develop and implement a strict password policy for your organisation. This should form part of a wider computer usage policy, which would also define acceptable usage for computer resources and email.

At the very least, your password policy should specify:

- Passwords should be as strong as possible.

- They should not be disclosed to anyone.

- They should be changed regularly.

When you implement your password policy, you should explain to people why it is important that they use strong passwords and change them regularly.

Hackers have a range of tools to help them to guess passwords. These include software that will literally enter a dictionary, one word at a time, in an attempt to gain access to a system. If the user's password is a simple word, or name, the hacker will almost certainly be able to access the system. Any actions undertaken will appear to be performed by the person whose password has been compromised.

It is good practice to change passwords regularly. At the very least, users should change their password after 90 days. Many computer systems and networks will support this by forcing users to change their password after a set amount of time.

It is also important that old passwords are not reused. Having a preferred password that is constantly used makes it easier to guess that password. Also, a previous password may have been compromised. Most computer systems help with this by storing a set number of previous passwords and not allowing people to reuse them. Sometimes, people try to get around this by changing their password multiple times in one sitting. The idea is to exhaust the number of stored passwords, so they can revert to the same password they have been using. Many systems also help to prevent this by allowing you to specify a maximum number of password changes that can be made in any one day.

You should always aim for users to comply with secure password policies by showing and illustrating the importance of the policy. There are also friendly password management tools and processes that can be used. A typical example is password synchronisation, which allows people to use one password for multiple systems in a network.

User authentication

If someone has lost their password, they may contact you to help them reset it. It is important to authenticate users in this case, to ensure the person is who they say they are.

Typically, people seeking to reset their password can be authenticated by using security measures such as biometric information or by answering one or more questions. Using personal questions is more common. When authenticating people by asking questions, you should ensure only that person will know the answers. You can do this by:

- Allowing users to set their own question and answer profiles.

- Defining standards for question and answer profiles, for example three questions, each of which has a different answer of ten or more characters.

- Asking a unique set of questions for each individual.

- Making the questions personal, so that only the true individual would know the answer.

- Asking users to answer different, randomly selected questions each time they need to authenticate.

- Specifying a set number of failed authentication attempts that will lock the account and trigger a security incident.

Create a strong password

The strength of a password relates to how easy or difficult it might be to guess or decipher. The stronger a password is, the more secure it will be. However, it is also important that people can remember their passwords.

Stronger passwords contain more than ten characters and consist of random letters, numbers and special characters (these are characters on a keyboard that are not letters or numbers. Typical examples include: £ % @ : *).

This makes the password hard to guess or decipher. However, this also makes the password hard to remember. If someone cannot remember their password easily, they will often write it down somewhere, which poses a security threat.

If there is no policy on password strength, people will often use simple words as passwords, which are easy to guess.

Most security guidance recommends that passwords are between seven and eight characters long and consist of random letters, numbers and special characters. This provides a compromise between ensuring passwords are strong and that people can remember them.

To create a strong, but memorable password:

- Ensure it contains at least seven or eight characters, or longer if the user will be able to remember it.

- Use a random combination of upper and lower case letters as well as numbers and special characters.

- Try to ensure the password is memorable for the person, but not easy to guess or, should it be found.

Avoid a weak password

Weak passwords are often more memorable, so people are inclined to use them. However, they are also often more easily guessed. Examples of weak passwords include:

- The same letter repeated, such as 'fffff'.

- Simple words or phrases, such as 'password'.

- Words that appear in a dictionary, even if the word is chosen at random.

- Proper names, for example a friend, family member or pet.

- Other names, such as product names, etc.

- Names or words, with numbers exchanged for letters, such as "B1ll" (for Bill).

- Letters or numbers in order, such as "abcd".

- A series of letters as they appear on a keyboard, such as "asdfqwerty".

- Personal numbers, such as a phone number or licence plate.

- Birth dates.

Protect passwords from misuse

Once a password has been set, it is vital that it is kept secret so that others cannot use or misuse it. There are a number of guidelines that should be followed to ensure a password is not compromised. You should share these with everyone in your organisation.

Passwords should be kept secret. If it seems someone knows or has guessed a password, it should be changed immediately.

As mentioned earlier, passwords should not be written down. However, if someone feels the need to do this, they should keep the password somewhere secure and not on their person.

Users should know to only enter passwords to trusted systems and websites. If something seems wrong, they should not enter a password.

User permissions, accounts and groups

Defining user groups within a small IT network environment helps organise users who may be logically connected or considered as a group. A user group is a set of user which accounts share the same kinds of access rights, and security permissions.

The users may work together as part of a team or department, share various resources, or who may use the same kinds of tools such as files, applications and printers.

As such, many of the group will have the same kinds of resource requirements. For this reason it is often sensible to set users up with their own accounts, which provide for their access and security, and as part of a user group, where they share rights and resources in common with other network users.

An important role for a network administrator is to specify any group structure, to provide the necessary folders and access permissions in line with the hierarchy which is established, and then to manage the user group authorisations that go along with this.

In this section, common resources, user and group permissions as well as troubleshooting issues, are covered.

Permission types

There are six standard permission types which apply to files and folders in Windows:

- *Full Control*: this is where users can access and view file names within folders and subfolders. They can open, read, write to, save, or delete files. With this permission users can add files to folders or subfolders, delete folders or subfolders, as well as change permissions and access rights to files and folders.

- *Modify:* users in this permissions category can access and view file names within folders and subfolders. They can open, read, write to, and save files. With this permission users can add files to folders or subfolders, and view the properties associated with files and folder.

- *Read and Execute:* users in this permissions category can access and view file names within folders and subfolders. They can open and read files. With this permission users can view folder and file properties, and view permissions.

- *List Folder Contents:* users can view folders. They can open and read files. With this permission users can navigate throughout subfolders in the folder, and view folder properties and permissions.

- *Read:* users can access folders, view file names and subfolder names. They can navigate to different subfolders, and view folder properties and permissions. Users can also copy data and view data.

- *Write:* users can create new folders, add files, change file properties and view folder permissions.

Each of these permission types describes specific actions that a person is allowed to perform on their computer. These are described below.

Full Control permits the user to:

- View file names and subfolders
- Open files
- Navigate to subfolders
- View folder and file properties
- Add files and subfolders to the folder
- Change the folder's files
- Delete the folder and its files
- View and change permissions
- Take ownership of the folder and its files

Modify permits the user to:

- View file names and subfolders
- Open files
- Navigate to subfolders
- View folder and file properties
- Add files and subfolders to the folder
- Change the folder's files
- View permissions

Read and Execute permits the user to:

- View file names and subfolders
- Open files
- Navigate to subfolders
- View folder and file properties
- View permissions

List Folder Contents permits the user to:

- View folders
- Open files
- Navigate to subfolders
- View folder properties
- View permissions

Read permits the user to:

- View the file names and subfolder names
- Navigate to subfolders
- View folder and file properties
- View permissions
- Copy and view data in the folder's files

Write permits the user to:

- Create folders
- Add new files
- Modify file properties
- View permissions

Applying permissions to folder

You apply permissions to a folder on a computer or network from the folder's *Properties* dialogue box. To access this dialogue box, right-click on the folder and click *Properties*.

When defining permissions for folders, you need to determine who will be allowed to access the folder.

It is important to keep your permissions straightforward. If someone has access to a folder, but not to the folder in which it is stored, this can cause problems. Similarly, if someone has full access to a folder, but not to a folder within it, there can be confusion, as the system may not apply the permissions in the manner you intend.

To define the permissions for a folder:

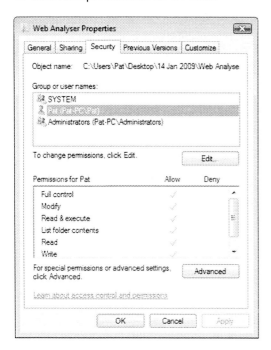

Actions

▶ 1. Access the *Properties* dialogue box by right-clicking on the folder.

▶ 2. Select the *Security* tab and click the *Edit* button.

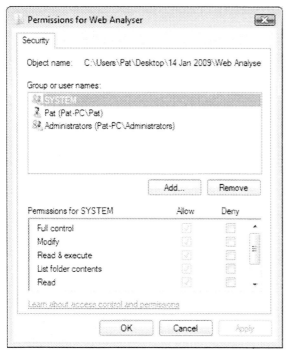

Actions

▶ 3. Click *Edit*. The *Permissions* dialog box appears.

▶ 4. Click *Add*. The *Select Users, Computers, or Groups* dialogue box appears.

▶ 5. In this dialogue box, you define the objects that you want to provide permissions for.

▶ 6. Type the name of the object in the field at the bottom of the dialogue box. Click *Check Names* to ensure the names are recognised, and click *OK*.

To allow a new group or user to access the folder, click the *Add* button. This opens the *Select Users or Groups* dialogue box.

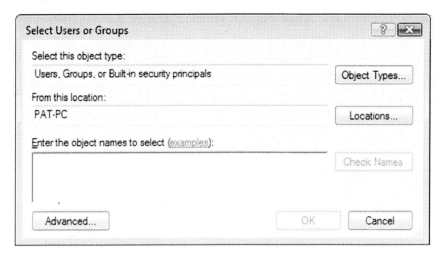

Setting permissions

Once you have granted a group or individual user access to a folder, you will need to set permissions for the new user(s). When you set permissions, you are specifying what level of access users have to the folder and the files within it.

Folder permissions can only be changed by:

- An administrator.

- The user that created the folder.

- A user who has been granted rights to change folder permissions.

Click on a user or group name to define permissions for them. The permissions currently assigned to them will be displayed in the lower pane of the *Permissions* dialogue box.

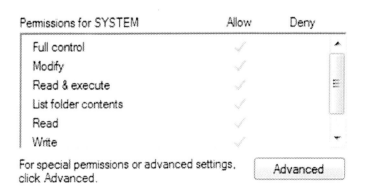

Actions

▶ 1. In the *Permissions* section, use the check boxes to select the appropriate *Allow* and *Deny* permission level.

▶ 2. Click *OK*.

▶ 3. The new permissions are given to the selected user(s) or group(s).

User groups in Windows

> A user group is a collection of accounts that have the same security permissions applied to them.

Assigning users to a group makes it quick and easy to assign permissions for network resources, such as shared folders, printers, etc. By assigning permission to the group, you assign permission to each account within the group.

An important task for the Network Administrator is to carefully record the members of groups and the group permissions.

To create a new group, you need to access *Groups* in the *Microsoft Management Console*. Use the following steps to do this:

Actions

▶ 1. Click *Start*.

▶ 2. Type 'mmc' into the *Search* box to launch the *Microsoft Management Console*.

▶ 3. Click *Local Users and Groups* in the left pane. If you do not see this option, use these steps to create it:

    a. Click *File*, select *Add/Remove Snap-in*.
    b. Click *Local Users and Groups* in the list.
    c. Click *Add*.
    d. Click *Local computer*.
    e. Click *Finish*.
    f. Click *OK*.

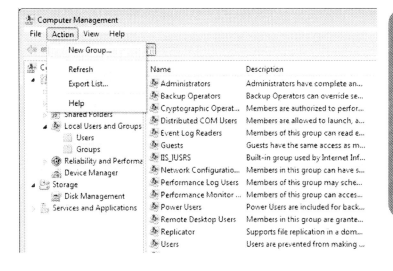

Actions

▶ 4. Once you have accessed the *Groups* folder, you can create a new group. Click *Action* and select *New Group* to do this.

▶ 5. In the *New Group* dialogue box type a group name and a description.

Actions

▶ 6. Click *Add*, and then type the name of the user account.

▶ 7. Click *OK*.

▶ 8. Click *Create*.

Additional members can be removed or added to a group at any stage following the same procedural approach.

Malicious software and antivirus software

Malicious software, also known as malware, is the name given to a range of applications that are intended to cause disruption, steal, copy, manipulate or destroy information or applications on a computer. The most common types of malware are:

- Viruses

- Trojan horses

- Worms

- Spyware

- SPAM

Viruses

A virus is so called because it can infect a computer and replicate itself without your knowledge or consent. Viruses require some user action to start, but they are generally hidden in trusted applications for example, Microsoft Word or Excel. Viruses generally cause disruption by slowing system resources or destroying information stored on a computer. They can also send information to others.

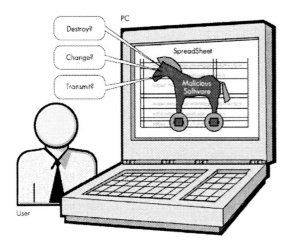

Trojan horse

Trojan horses are so called because they appear to be legitimate applications and are only activated when you run them.

They can be installed by accident, while installing another application, or by posing as some other kind of application. Trojan horses cause disruption in a variety of ways. They can read, copy, alter or destroy information on your computer, allow someone to access your computer remotely, and send details of your activity to others.

Worms

Worms are so called because they burrow through a network, replicating themselves and sending themselves to other computers. They do not require your intervention to operate and will often go unnoticed for quite some time. Early Worm types did not alter the systems they passed through. However, more recent Worms have been known to include a 'payload', which does perform some action. Payloads can include deleting information on a computer, gathering information to send to a third party, using an email account to send SPAM and even providing remote control of the computer to someone else.

Spyware

Spyware is so called because once installed on your computer, it will monitor your activity. Sometimes, they will even provide control of the computer or resources to a third party over the Internet. As with all malicious software, spyware is generally installed secretly and without your consent. Spyware can be used for a range of purposes, from gathering personal data or login information to sending details of a users personal activity to someone who then sends unsolicited advertisements to you based on this.

SPAM

Spam is the name given to unsolicited emails sent to a large number of recipients. They are usually of a commercial nature. This is not considered to be malicious software. However, the majority of malicious software is now transmitted through SPAM messages. Email security will be discussed in more detail later.

Malicious software distribution

Malicious software is distributed using a variety of methods. These include:

- As attachments to emails.

- Using network resources.

- Tricking users into running an installation application from a website.

- Pretending to be some other kind of application that a user downloads and installs.

- On portable storage media and devices, such as USB keys and CDs/DVDs.

To protect against viruses in your organisation, you should install a network and personal firewall on all computers. You should also ensure that antivirus software is installed on every computer and that it is updated regularly.

You should share the following advice with everyone in your organisation:

- Only download and install software from trusted sources (you may want to prevent people from downloading and installing software altogether, if it is practical).

- Scan USB keys and network resources regularly (most antivirus software can be set up to do this automatically).

- Users should know to never open an email attachment that they are not expecting to receive. Worms can send themselves through email accounts. If a user receives an attachment they were not expecting, or that has a strange name, they should be instructed to contact the network administrator.

You can also:

- Ensure a firewall is in place, regularly updated and working properly.

- Block access to Peer to Peer (P2P) websites, where each computer can act as both client and server. Your firewall can help you do this.

- If practical, prevent users from installing software onto their computers.

- If practical, prevent users from installing hardware on their computers.

- Educate users in your organisation about the dangers of malicious software and how easily it can spread.

Antivirus software

You need to install antivirus software on any computer you have control of or responsibility for.

Despite its name, antivirus software is generally designed to seek out any form of malicious software (not just viruses) and deal with it.

There is a large variety of antivirus software available, some even free. However, it is good practice to buy a reliable paid version of antivirus software when protecting an organisation's network. For paid versions, you usually pay for the software itself, then pay an annual fee to keep it updated.

It is important to keep your antivirus software updated as malicious software is released every day. To effectively protect your network, your antivirus software needs to know what to look for and how to deal with it. It will only know this by being updated daily. You may need to configure personal and network firewalls to allow antivirus software to access, download and install new updates.

Laws and Guidelines

Data protection legislation

National data protection legislation defines the legal basis for the handling of personal information in a particular country and provides the basis by which individuals can govern the control of information about themselves. Such legislation typically confers rights on individuals who have their personal information stored as well as obligations on those who store such data.

The principles of data protection require that personal data should be processed fairly and lawfully. In order for data to be classed as fairly processed, at least one of the following six conditions must be applicable to the data:

- The data subject (the person whose data is stored) has consented to the processing.

- Processing is necessary for the performance of a contract (any processing not directly required to complete a contract would not be fair).

- Processing is required under a legal obligation (other than one stated in the contract).

- Processing is necessary to protect the vital interests of the data subject's rights.

- Processing is necessary to carry out any public functions.

- Processing is necessary in order to pursue the legitimate interests of the data controller or third parties (unless it could unjustifiably prejudice the interests of the data subject).

You should be aware of the applicable legislation in your own country.

Copyright laws and the Internet

Copyright material published on the Internet will generally be protected in the same way as material in other media. Copyright is protected internationally through international treaties, such as, the Berne Convention to which over 160 countries are parties to. Before the Berne Convention, national copyright laws usually only applied for works created within each country.

Copyright has two main purposes, namely the protection of the author's right to obtain commercial benefit from valuable work and the protection of the author's general right to control how a work is used. Almost all works are copyrighted the moment they are written and no copyright notice is required.

You should be aware that if publishing material from other sources the express permission of the copyright owner (unless copyright exceptions apply) is required. In all cases, copies should be acknowledged as far as is practicable. In addition, many websites will include a copyright statement setting out exactly the way in which materials on the site may be used.

You should also be aware that many online resources may have been published illegally without the permission of the copyright owners. Any subsequent use of the materials, such as printing, or copying and pasting, may also be illegal.

For further details on copyright requirements within your own country please refer to your own applicable national legislation.

Health issues and ergonomics

Ergonomics is the scientific discipline concerned with designing according to human needs in order to optimise human well-being and overall system performance.

A little knowledge of the principles of ergonomics, how users interact safely and efficiently with computers and their work environment, can save a lot of discomfort and maximise both productivity and enjoyment.

Given the increasing amount of time spent by users at computer workstations either at work or at home users, need to be aware of their own personal ergonomics and how can avoid or reduce the risk of personal injury.

The risk of personal injury associated with the use of computers can be reduced by giving careful consideration to the following:

- Ensuring an adequate work area for equipment, materials as well as adequate personal work space.

- Ensuring proper chair and work top heights. The chair should be fully adjustable with adequate back and arm rest supports. The work top should have adequate height clearance from the user's legs.

- Monitors should be adjustable, positioned away from glaring lights or fitted with an appropriate anti-glare guard to reduce glare, properly positioned with regard to eye level and distance so as to reduce eye strain, neck and shoulder pain and fatigue.

- The keyboard and mouse should be properly positioned so as to avoid awkward posture and undue strain on shoulders, elbows, forearms, wrists and hands. There are quite a few ergonomically designed keyboard and mice now available to reduce potential risks and strains in this regard.

- Users should take frequent short breaks (every 30-40 minutes) to reduce eye and muscle strain and allow the body to recover.

Users should be aware of their organisation's policy with regard to health and safety issues associated with the use of personal computers, which should relate to the ergonomic principles highlighted above.

Ventilation

The case of a computer is the metallic box which houses the various internal components. Cases also have other uses, such as blocking noise produced by the computer, and protection from electromagnetic radiation.

A case houses all of the computer's internal electronic components. Sometimes, a computer's electronics can reach very high temperatures. For this reason, you must choose a case with good ventilation, meaning that it has as many fans as possible, as well as air vents on the side to allow hot air to escape. It is recommended, that you choose a case which includes at least an air intake in front, a removable air filter, and an air outlet in the rear.

Most of the components in a computer produce heat. The hot air from this heat moves upwards to the power supply. The power supply unit that comes with a computer case includes a fan (or fans) within the unit, which is designed to draw out the hot air and expel it to the exterior, keeping the computer cool. The power supply unit helps maintain air flow thereby reducing a build up of heat in the computer.

Computers should be inspected for dust accumulation at least once every three months. Before inspecting a computer, turn off the power and unplug the power cord from the electrical outlet, then remove any dust from vents and perforations in the front panel. If you notice external dust accumulation, then examine and remove dust from the inside of the computer including heat sink inlet fins, power supply vents, and fans. Always turn off and unplug the computer before opening the cover.

For safety and to maintain optimum computer performance, users should always follow these basic precautions with a desktop computer:

- Keep the cover closed whenever the computer is plugged in.

- Regularly inspect the outside of the computer for dust accumulation.

- Remove dust from vents and any perforations in the bezel. More frequent cleanings might be required for computers in dusty or high-traffic areas.

- Do not restrict or block any ventilation openings.

- Do not store or operate the computer inside furniture, as this might increase the risk of overheating.

You should remember when using a laptop that ventilation slots and fans are provided for safety and comfort as well as reliable operation. Avoid using laptops on sofas or beds as the ventilation slots and fans may become obstructed and lead to a build-up of excessive heat. Users should also avoid leaving their laptop in contact with their lap for any extended period of time as extended contact could result in skin burn and, in extreme cases, even possible loss of fertility among males.

Eye care

There is no evidence that working at a computer damages eyes, however, long hours working in front of a computer can be fatiguing and there are a number of tips users can follow to minimise the effects of fatigue:

- Taking frequent 'eye breaks' to give eyes a rest. Looking at a monitor for long periods causes users to blink less often resulting in dryer eyes. Users should look away from the monitor every 15 minutes or so and blink rapidly for a few seconds to refresh the tear film.

- Ensure a monitor is at a comfortable distance from the eyes (40cm – 60cm) and that the centre of the screen is (approximately 15cm) below their natural eye level.

- Monitor glare from various light sources can also be a problem. To counter this, ensure that your screen is positioned so that windows and lights are to the side of the screen. Newer monitors reduce glare. If using an older monitor fit an antiglare screen.

- Users should have a routine eye test every two years. Sometimes users may be entitled to have a routine eye test paid for by their employer.

Secure cabling

Health and safety considerations require due care to be taken in relation to the positioning and securing of cables used with computing equipment. Particular issues to be aware of are as follows:

- Cover and secure trailing power cables. Route power cables so that desk chairs, trolleys and other objects do not roll over them, and so that they will not be walked on, tripped over, or pinched by objects.

- Replace frayed leads or damaged plugs. Use only the power cables and power adapters approved by the product manufacturer for use with your particular product.

- Do not overload circuits, particularly when using long extension leads, as power surging can occur if too many computers are connected to a circuit.

- Avoid coiled cables, as the heat generated within them could be sufficient to start a fire.

- Be aware of accidental damage, in particular any cuts to power cable insulation.

- Ensure that keyboard, mouse and printer connecting cables do not hang over the front of the computer workstation. Where the workstations are accessible from the rear ensure that trailing loops of cable are tidied to allow easy access to equipment for maintenance and to prevent equipment from being dragged accidentally from the workstation.

Disability / equality legislation

Disability legislation prohibits direct discrimination, victimisation and harassment and promotes equality for disabled people. Disability legislation, in particular, makes it unlawful to discriminate against people in respect of their disabilities in relation to such matters as employment, the provision of goods and services, education and transport.

At national level, policies relating to people with disabilities reflect the diversity of cultures and legislative frameworks in the EU Member States. The definitions and the criteria for determining disability are currently laid down in national legislation and administrative practices and differ across the current Member States according to their perceptions of, and approaches to, disability.

Users should be aware of their own applicable national legislation as well as relevant international directives.

Quick Quiz

Select the correct answer from the following multiple-choice questions:

1   Which accessibility feature is designed for people who have difficulty holding two or more keys down at once?

    a   StickyKeys

    b   FilterKeys

    c   ToggleKeys

    d   SoundSentry

2   Which type of server generally handles outgoing email?

    a   FTP

    b   POP3

    c   HTTP

    d   SMTP

3   Which of the following would be regarded as the strongest password formulation?

    a   Document

    b   ABCDEF

    c   %TaDLic56

    d   08082008

4   What type of malware may send browsing information back to advertisers to target the user with unsolicited adverts?

    a   Trojan horse

    b   Worm

    c   SPAM

    d   Spyware

5   As a minimum, how often should a computer user look away from their monitor? Every:

a   5 – 8 minutes

b   10 – 15 minutes

c   30 minutes

d   60 minutes

Answers to Quick Quiz

1   a   StickyKeys

2   b   SMTP

3   d   %TaDLic56

4   d   Spyware

5   b   10 – 15 minutes